CCH BUSINESS OWNER'S TOOLKIT™

LAUNCHING YOUR FIRST SMALL BUSINESS

MAKE THE RIGHT DECISIONS DURING YOUR FIRST 90 DAYS

Second Edition

A *CCH Business Owner's Toolkit*™ Publication

Edited by John L. Duoba
and Paul Gada, J.D., LL.M., M.B.A.

CCH INCORPORATED
Chicago
A WoltersKluwer Company

Consumer Media Group
CCH INCORPORATED
2700 Lake Cook Road
Riverwoods, Illinois 60015

This publication is designed to provide accurate and authoritative information in regard to the subject matter covered. It is sold with the understanding that the publisher is not engaged in rendering legal, accounting, or other professional service, and that the authors are not offering such advice in this publication. If legal advice or other expert assistance is required, the services of a competent professional should be sought.

Cover designed by Tim Kaage, Laurel Graphx, Inc.

Books may be purchased at quantity discounts for educational, business or sales promotion use. For more information please contact:

Consumer Media Group
CCH INCORPORATED
2700 Lake Cook Road
Riverwoods, Illinois 60015

ISBN 0-8080-0859-5

Printed in the United States of America

THE CCH BUSINESS OWNER'S TOOLKIT TEAM

Drew Snider, Publisher, Consumer Media Group (*dsnider@cch.com*) has over 25 years experience with business-information services (SRDS), consumer magazines (*Golfweek*), and home-based software applications (Parsons Technology).

Alice H. Magos (*amagos@cch.com*) has over 35 years of experience running the operations of numerous small businesses. She is the author of the *CCH Business Owner's Toolkit*™ online advice column "Ask Alice." Alice is a popular instructor at small business seminars on accounting, financial planning, and using the Internet; is an accountant and a Certified Financial Planner; and holds degrees from Washington University in St. Louis and Northwestern University.

Joel Handelsman (*jhandels@cch.com*) has almost 25 years of experience writing about business, tax, and financial topics. He has been involved in multiple new product and business ventures in the publishing industry, and has held a variety of management positions. Joel holds degrees from Northwestern University's Medill School of Journalism and DePaul University College of Law.

John L. Duoba (*jduoba@cch.com*) has more than 15 years of small business experience in book and magazine publishing, fulfilling various roles in editorial and production management. He has been involved in the publication of scores of titles, with multiple editions and issues raising the total well into the hundreds. John is a professional journalist and holds a degree from Northwestern University's Medill School of Journalism.

Paul N. Gada (*pgada@cch.com*) has over eight years of legal publishing experience, primarily in dealing with federal and state tax issues. He has helped create numerous editorial products, including newsletters, journals, books and electronic information systems. Paul is an attorney and holds degrees from the John Marshall Law School (LLM. - Tax and Employee Benefits), Southern Illinois University (JD), Northern Illinois University (MBA) and Loyola University of Chicago (BA).

Catherine Gordon (*cgordon@cch.com*) has over 15 years of experience in the tax, business, and financial publishing field and has worked as a tax consultant providing services to individuals as well as large and small companies. Catherine holds a juris doctorate degree from the State University of New York at Buffalo School of Law and a BA in sociology from the State University of New York at Stony Brook.

We would also like to acknowledge the significant efforts of Susan M. Jacksack, J.D., for her contributions to this book.

FOREWORD

Welcome to the world of self-employment! With the rapid increase in current technology and the growth of the global community, small businesses are now able to compete in our economy as at no other time in our history. And the numbers back it up. According to government statistics, new small business formation reaches record levels each year. Currently, more than 23 million small businesses in the U.S. make up 99.7 percent of all employers and 53 percent of the private work force.

Yes, opportunity abounds, but nothing is handed to these entrepreneurs. Gaining a foothold in the marketplace can be difficult for a startup operation. Still, there are many, many success stories, and they all share some common qualities: thorough research and planning, skillful management, and the necessary financial resources. When running such a business, the margin for error is small and there may not be time for a second chance.

Written by a special team of small business experts, accountants and attorneys, *Launching Your First Small Business*—now in its second edition—provides you with the information you need to successfully make the transition to self-employment. With coverage of topics like assessing personal strengths and weaknesses, matching those skills to the right opportunity, considering the costs to open and run your new venture for the first 90 days, selecting professionals, choosing an organizational form, business planning and marketing your concept, and equipping and staffing the right facility and location, this complete resource will help you make more informed management decisions. And well-thought-out decisions will keep your business on a path to success.

Why should you turn to us? **CCH** INCORPORATED is a leading provider of information and software to the business and professional community. More than four generations of business advisors have trusted our products, and now you can too.

A caution and an invitation—the discussions of the laws contained in this book are current as of the date of publication. But remember, things change. So, as you run and grow your business, keep abreast of the latest news by visiting the *CCH Business Owner's Toolkit* on the Internet (www.toolkit.cch.com). Take a look at the interactive information and tools we offer to assist you in running your business. While online, you also can ask follow-up questions of our team of small business experts, or you can visit our bookstore and peruse the library of titles offering guidance to small business owners on varying topics of interest. We welcome and look forward to your questions and comments.

Drew Snider

Publisher, Consumer Media Group

Table of Contents

Table of Contents

Part I

Clearing The Preliminary Hurdles

Thinking of starting your own business? You're not alone. Each year, thousands of people strike out on their own. Some have a great idea for a new business that they *know* will be a smashing success. Others just know that they're tired of being employees, helping someone else's business become a success.

Being your own boss brings with it a unique blend of freedom, opportunity and challenge that you're unlikely to experience in any other way. It also brings with it risk, hard work and a whole new set of responsibilities. Nevertheless, a growing number of people each year take on the challenges posed by starting a new business.

Yet, despite the best efforts of these budding new business owners, as many as one-third of all new small businesses fail. Why? The easy answers are poor management and not enough money. The former is generally a result of the owners lacking one or more of the skills critical to success. The latter frequently results from the failure to understand how much it will cost to start a business or from overly optimistic projections regarding income in the early days of the business.

How do you avoid these traps? Careful analysis and planning from the very beginning will surely help. You don't want to make decisions based on faulty assumptions, and you certainly don't want to find out that, even if your business works out, it doesn't provide you with the personal satisfaction or financial rewards you sought. Those businesses that do succeed, however, provide their owners with both financial rewards and the satisfaction of knowing they did it themselves.

How do you make sure your new business is among those that enjoy the kind of success you hope for? What distinguishes the winners from the also-rans? The purpose of this book is to take you through the critical process of starting a new business, one step at a time. From the moment you start thinking that launching your own business might be a realistic alternative, through the time you open your doors for the first time, to the first 90 days of operation, you'll explore many options and make some tough decisions. We're here to see to it that you pick the best options and make informed, intelligent decisions. We can't guarantee you success, but we can put you in a position to truly take your best shot.

In this first part of the book, we'll examine the conditions and environment necessary for an entrepreneur to make the decision to step out on his or her own.

Chapter 1: Are You Ready To Be Your Own Boss? provides the information you need to make a frank assessment of whether you should start your own business. Special emphasis is placed on the key characteristics and qualities of those who succeed. It continues with a review of how you can expect your life to change when you choose to start a new business.

Chapter 2: The Right Small Business for You explains how to decide what *type* of business to open. Forty years ago, most new businesses dealt in goods, manufacturing or other tangible products. Today, an increasing number of new small businesses are service providers. Whatever you choose, it's clear that you need to find a business that matches your skills and preferences.

Chapter 3: Can You Afford To Go Into Business? looks at your personal financial needs and resources. It helps you establish the sources of your income and the uses to which it will be put. In addition, we'll look at some of the potential sources of capital for people starting a new business.

Chapter 1

Are You Ready To Be Your Own Boss?

People who start their own businesses can be grouped into two broad categories. The first group consists of people who know exactly what they want to do and are merely looking for the opportunity or resources to do it. Usually, these people have already developed many of the skills necessary to succeed in their chosen field. They are also likely to be familiar with industry customs and practices, which can help during the startup phase of a new business.

The second group consists of people who want to start their own business, but don't have any real definite ideas about what they'd like to do. While these people have developed skills in the course of their employment or education, they may not be interested in opening a business in the same field of endeavor.

How you proceed will depend, in large part, on which group you're in. For those who know what they want to do, the task is a bit easier. There's no need to research business ideas and opportunities to decide which might be suitable. Instead, these folks can jump right in and assess their chances for success in the type of business they've selected.

Those who merely want out of the traditional corporate world have an extra step: choosing a suitable type of business. One logical starting point is to think about what it is you like to do. Many businesses serve people pursuing their hobbies and interests. If you have a strong interest in something, think about the needs of other people who share your interests. Is there something you can provide? It may help to think in terms of *goods* and *services*. Most businesses involve a mixture of both, but this dichotomy can help narrow the focus.

Example

John's a house painter who has been working for the same employer for 12 years. Although he started out as a helper, John now prepares the estimates and bids on jobs. He's experienced, has all of his own tools and equipment, and has been doing side jobs on weekends for some time. John believes he has enough contacts and referrals to provide full-time work. From his perspective, his employer is just a middleman, standing between John and his potential customers, and reaping the benefits of John's hard work. He believes the time is right to start his own house painting business.

Another approach is to consider the skills you've developed over the years, both on the job and at home. Do friends or associates come to you when they have computer problems? Does everyone you know ask your advice when they're shopping for a car? Do you have a workshop in the basement? Consider all of these in terms of what marketable goods or services you can provide.

By far, you are the most important single factor in the success or failure of your business. Unfortunately, not everyone who wants to run a small business is actually capable of doing it. Earlier, we mentioned most small business failures are the result of poor management or insufficient money. Therefore, let's start by taking the steps necessary to reduce your risk of failure from these and other causes.

Example

Kathy has been working for a marketing firm ever since she graduated from college six years ago. Although she hasn't run into a glass ceiling, she knows she won't be able earn what she'd like, even if she continues to rise within the company. And the work, once exciting, has now gotten old. She'd very much like to do something else, but determining what it will be is an open issue. She's sure she doesn't want to work for someone else anymore, and she'd like to do something other than marketing.

WHAT DO YOU WANT FROM SELF-EMPLOYMENT?

Surprisingly, answering this question isn't as easy as it sounds. Sure, you want to be your own boss and enjoy the rewards that come from running a successful business. But what does that involve? Can you be specific in describing what you want to spend your time doing and what you hope to achieve?

For many people, it helps to translate these expectations and desires into concrete terms by setting goals. We've organized these into three broad categories: economic goals, personal goals and retirement goals.

The last item might seem a bit out of place, but it's vital for everyone, employee and entrepreneur alike, to recognize there'll come a time when you want to kick back and enjoy the fruits of your labor. In this time of growing concern over the continued viability of the Social Security system, any goal-setting you do should involve consideration of your needs *after* you've built and run your business.

Goals won't just determine whether you start a small business, they'll also play a prominent role in just about every decision you make along the way. Decisions relating to how you structure your business, whether you hire employees, and how you market your products or services must all be measured against one thing: Will this course of action help me achieve my goals? Remember, goals aren't just the destination you're driving toward, they're also the painted white lines keeping you on the road.

Example

You currently earn $35,000 a year, but you hate your job and yearn to leave. You have an idea for a small business that involves servicing a small niche market, and you set a goal of being recognized as the expert in that niche area within five years. You analyze your idea and discover that, while no one else is servicing that market, it's a small market and you're not likely to make more than $25,000 for at least the first three years. But you also believe that, because your business is unique and your chances of becoming a recognized expert are good, you'll have much greater income potential after the first three years. Despite the probable cut in income for three years, you decide the risks are worth it, so you'll start the new business.

Economic Goals

Obviously, you want your business to be a success. But how you define success depends on a number of personal factors. Assuming you've been in the work force for a while, you know what kind of lifestyle you can afford on your current income. If you're like most people, you'd probably like to earn more. Many people feel that self-employment is the way to do it.

Sometimes, it's economic *pressures* that cause a person to consider opening a new business:

- **Increase earnings** — Some people believe working as an employee in a corporate setting limits their earning potential, and they want the chance to make the kind of money they feel they deserve.

- **Replace earnings** — Some people have been downsized or

rightsized, or whatever it's called these days, and they need to replace their lost income.

- **Supplement earnings** — Changed family circumstances may require a second source of income, which translates into a part-time business.

In setting economic goals, remember that most businesses don't immediately produce profits for the owner. Be realistic about how long it will be before your new business becomes an established and secure source of income (see Chapter 10).

Personal Goals

Money isn't the whole story, at least for most people. There's a certain satisfaction in "doing it yourself" that may not be quantifiable, but which is nevertheless important. Typical reasons that people choose to start a business include:

- **Freedom** — Some people just don't like working for others, and they want the freedom to make their own decisions. Owning your own business is a way to achieve personal freedom on many levels.

- **Career change** — Most people change jobs or even careers several times during the course of their lives. Sometimes, it's by choice; other times, existing jobs simply disappear.

- **Satisfaction** — Some people feel trapped in a field they don't enjoy, and they want a chance to work at something they find more interesting.

- **Recognition** — Being an expert or authority in a particular field is also an important factor for many people. They don't just want to start a business; they want to be recognized for the quality of their work and their expertise.

- **Flexibility** — Self-employed people have more freedom to choose businesses allowing them to satisfy personal preferences, such as working outdoors, maintaining hours other than 9 to 5, having seasonal vacations, etc.

- **Responsibility** — Some feel lost in a corporate setting, and they want the chance to play a bigger role in their chosen field.

- **Professional growth** — Some people believe their ideas are being ignored or not being used properly in a corporate setting, and they want the chance to do it the "right" way.

- **Benefits and security** — With corporations looking for ways to control costs, the benefits offered to employees aren't as plentiful as they once were. Many people feel the traditional advantages of working for a large employer are gone. Retirement plans are increasingly less generous, corporate health plans are costing employees more each year, and the job security corporate workers once enjoyed has been greatly reduced.

Retirement Goals

Most people look forward to a time when they can relax and enjoy themselves without the need to work. The chance to do just what you want, when you want to do it, is a strong motivator. Admittedly, some people still choose to work because they want to work—they enjoy it. In fact, lots of successful small business owners keep working into their 70s and 80s. However, the vast majority of people look forward to retirement. Many strive to make it happen sooner rather than later.

Anyone who has spoken with a personal financial planner knows it takes a lot of money to retire and live comfortably. Many people believe they can do a better job of ensuring they'll have enough money for retirement if they're in charge of the source of their income.

In addition, a successful small business can provide more than just steady income saved for the future. Prior to retirement, you may be able to sell your thriving operation for a nice profit. Or you could sell ownership interests to others, who then will run the business while you collect a share of the profits.

Setting Goals

Most of us are not strongly motivated by money itself. Before you reject this statement out of hand, think of this: Unless you are a coin or currency collector, the thrill of having $5,000,000 in a locked vault would quickly wear off if you couldn't spend it or use it in any way. In much the same way, a purely monetary goal may not be a very powerful motivator: Most of us need to focus on tangible items or tangible benefits that money can buy. (Despite this statement, some people are motivated by money and are moved to action by the numbers. If you're such a person, you can move right on to the discussion of making the goals measurable.)

But for most of us, one of the first steps in goal-setting is finding a concrete goal or goals that motivate us emotionally. How about that powder-blue '57 Chevy convertible, the retirement on Maui, the ability to cut back on working hours, or the satisfaction from setting up and funding your own charitable foundation? Spend a day or two making a list of the things you've always wanted, then prioritizing them. You'll probably find you have some short-term and some long-term goals.

Moreover, make sure these are your goals, not someone else's, or the goals you *think* you should want. If you're not honest with yourself about what you want, when the going gets rough, you will find it harder to have the self-discipline to stick to the plan needed to attain the goal.

Once you have a list of the goals that will motivate you, don't let the dream die. If you haven't done so already, do enough research on your goal so that you know it inside and out. At least once a day, imagine what it would be like to have your goal and how your life would be improved. If the goal can be represented by a picture (such as the '57 Chevy), keep one or more pictures of it where you're bound to notice it.

Isn't this just daydreaming? If you go no further with our suggested goal-setting process, these vivid imaginings *will* be little more than daydreams. Potentially, they can waste your time and, worse still, provide an excuse not to do those distasteful, but necessary things you must do to grow your business (such as, for instance, cold-calling prospective customers). To really derive any benefit from this exercise of envisioning your goals, you must make your goals measurable.

Quantifying Your Goals

Soul-searching and honest self-examination can help you decide what you want from a new business. However, moving from general goals (e.g., financial security) to specific targets can be a long and difficult process. How much money represents financial security? What do you expect in terms of personal time, vacations, continuing education, etc.? What exactly does "a successful small business" mean to you? A national customer base? A certain magic number in sales, such as $1 million? Recognition as a community business leader?

You'll have to gather a lot of information before you're ready to set specific targets. Eventually, you'll probably want to put those goals together in the form of a business plan.

But before we move on to the process of getting that information, let's take a look at some guidelines that can help you establish goals that are meaningful and measurable.

- **Be specific** — Establish targets that can be easily measured, and use numbers as targets whenever possible. For example, you may set a goal of selling your goods or services across a particular geographic area, having a certain number of customers, or reaching a particular level of sales. Tie those numbers to specific time frames (within six months, within two years, within 10 years, etc.).

- **Be realistic** — Having high expectations is great, but you should establish targets that are reasonable and achievable. Don't open a fast-food restaurant with the expectation your business will be bigger than McDonald's within the first six months.

- **Be aggressive** — You can be realistic and still aim high. Don't set goals that are too easily achieved; also, set both short-term and long-term goals. If, after six months in business, you reach all of your goals, then what? Don't sell yourself short; if you want to be bigger than McDonald's within 20 years, go for it.

- **Be consistent** — Beware of inadvertently setting inconsistent goals. For example, a goal of growing fast enough to have three employees within two years might be inconsistent with a goal of earning a particular amount of money, if the cost of adding the employees ends up temporarily reducing your income below the target level. There is nothing wrong with having both goals. Just be aware of any potential conflict and establish priorities among your goals, defining which are most important.

Some people have a hard time setting goals because they just don't know where to start. If that applies to you, we suggest you start with an easily quantifiable goal. For example, maybe you want to increase your take-home pay by 50 percent after three years in business. Later, in Chapter 3, we provide easy-to-use charts that will help you organize your personal living expenses and see exactly what you're spending, just to live. Use it to figure out the amount of money you'll need to earn in order to cover your living expenses. Whether or not your new business will be your sole source of income, you'll still need to earn enough to make ends meet.

CAN YOU DO IT?

Regardless of your desire to go into business for yourself, if you lack needed skills, it's unlikely you'll succeed. There are two distinctly different roles you'll play while preparing to open and run your own small business. Each requires specific skills. On the one hand, you're the person who will be responsible for providing products or services to your customers. This is true whether you have employees or not. On the other hand, you also have to deal with all the activities that relate to running your business. You need to be able to handle both in order to succeed.

Since every business is unique (or should be), the specific skill set needed to provide products or services will vary. Do your best to gauge the scope of activities that make up the business. Be particularly careful not to overlook the less-enjoyable aspects of the business. And every business has a few.

Assessing Your Strengths

Successful small business owners know their strengths and weaknesses. They build their businesses around their strengths and compensate for their weaknesses. To succeed, you'll have to be able to identify what you do well and what you don't do so well.

As you evaluate yourself, be honest. You'll only hurt yourself if you're not. Also, don't panic if you discover you have weaknesses. Every small business owner has them. The key to success is not so much in having every skill (although that would help) as it is in finding ways to compensate for the weaknesses. Let's begin by looking at some of the characteristics that will help you succeed in a new business venture.

Essential Qualities for Owners

You can be successful even if you don't possess every skill needed to run a small business. However, there are certain qualities you should possess if you're to be successful:

- **Willingness to sacrifice** — You must be willing to accept the fact that, as a small business owner, you are the last one to be paid. Your bank, your vendors and your employees are all in line ahead of you and must be paid before you see any of the money. You must also be willing to sacrifice much of what may have been your free time. If you like working 9 to 5, knowing how much you'll make and taking three weeks of vacation every year, don't go into business for yourself.

- **Interpersonal skills** — As a small business owner, you have to be able to maintain cordial relationships with everyone who touches your business. If you thought getting along with your boss was tough, wait until you have to deal with suppliers, customers, employees, lawyers, accountants, government officials, salespeople and everybody who wants a piece of your time. Successful owners have the ability to work with all personality types and are able to find out from their customers what they like and don't like. Many business owners spend a lot of time on the telephone talking to people they don't know.

- **Leadership ability** — Successful owners understand others are looking to them to call the shots and make the hard decisions. Others will be looking to you for answers and direction, and if you're not ready for that responsibility, you probably shouldn't own a business.

- **Organizational skills** — Successful owners are able to keep track of everything happening in their business, set priorities and get things done. They know if they lose track of what's going on, they're sunk.

- **Intelligence** — We're not talking about the ability to score well on standardized tests. We're talking more about street smarts and common sense. Successful owners anticipate problems before they arise and take preemptive steps to avoid them. They also take the time to think through the situation when a crisis does arise.

- **Management ability** — Small business is all about managing relationships, with your customers or clients, with your employees, with your suppliers, with your accountant and lawyer, with your banker, and with your family. If you don't think you can effectively manage those relationships, you shouldn't start a new business.

- **Business experience** — Without some solid business experience, you're probably not going to be able to borrow any money. Your banker will want to know about your experience, not just in business, but in the same field as the business you're hoping to start. If you lack experience, go get it any way you can: volunteer at an existing business, or try to get a part-time or weekend job in the field.

- **Optimism** — How will you react when business isn't going as well as expected? A pessimist may fold the tent, but an optimist who believes in the business will keep going. Successful owners are people who can deal with setbacks or disappointments.

Use the preceding list to assess your own capabilities. Identify the areas in which you excel and the ones where you're not so strong. You're now in a position to consider how to compensate for any weaknesses you've identified.

Although these qualities are important to a small business's success, particularly to one just starting, not every owner of every successful business has had every one of the desired qualities. So there's hope for those of us who don't possess every quality. There are other factors involved that don't relate to personal characteristics, and these can also have a substantial impact on the fortunes of a new small business.

- **The unique idea** — If you've built a better mousetrap, they'll beat a path to your door, even if you're a poorly organized, pessimistic misanthrope.

- **The genius** — If you possess the gift of greatness, they'll not only overlook your weaknesses, they'll revel in them.

- **Blind luck** — The Small Business Hall of Fame contains more than a few stories of people who backed into success because of their incredibly good timing.

Compensating for Weaknesses

Everyone who makes an honest effort at self-evaluation identifies areas of weakness. That's to be expected. But a realistic appraisal puts you in a better position to judge whether or not to start a business. If you can find some way to compensate for the weaknesses you identify, don't let them stop you from pursuing your business idea.

Example

John, our painter friend, can tell you how many gallons of paint it takes to cover 1700 square feet of wall. He knows how many hours it takes to do the trim work on 21 windows, three exterior doors and two eight-foot garage doors. But he hasn't been able to balance his checkbook…ever. But then, neither can his boss, who pays a part-time bookkeeper to handle the business's books and an accountant to do tax returns. John can get the same type of help, or attend the local community college and take basic bookkeeping courses.

Since weaknesses tend to relate to the inability to do certain tasks, ask yourself if you can reasonably afford to pay someone else to handle those tasks. For example, if you don't like to sell, you can hire a salesman. Down the road, as you get further along in setting up your new business, you may determine the convenience of paying someone else to do the work is outweighed by the costs. But for now, all you have to do is identify whether someone else *could* do the work for you.

If you lack skills critical to the business, your best bet may be to partner up with someone whose skill set complements yours. For example, a person who likes working with people but not with numbers and forms may be a good match for someone who likes working with numbers but not with people.

Finding a good partner can be difficult. Most people partner up with those they know best, such as friends and family. But be aware that partnering with those you know best doesn't always work. Some marriages and friendships have been ruined by business partnerships, while others have been enriched by them. Finding a partner through others means, such as through a business association, is even more tenuous. The best advice is to be careful. Make sure there is a good match before you go into business with someone else.

Another possibility is to develop the traits and skills yourself. There are at least three ways to do this. The first is by trial and error. In other words, you'll develop the skills over time by learning from your mistakes. The downside to this approach is most small businesses won't give you much time or allow you to make many mistakes. If you benefit from trial and error, it'll usually be with the third or fourth new business you start.

The second method for developing skills is to take classes at a local business school. While classes may offer a wealth of valuable information, they can be expensive, may take a long time to complete, and normally don't offer much in terms of real-world experience. Another option is taking community college courses, which are usually inexpensive and may provide some practical skills.

The third method of skill-building is using a small business incubator to help you get started. Incubators are programs that provide you with hands-on advice, as well as office space and access to office equipment and supplies. They're usually sponsored by local governments or community development agencies, but there are some private ones as well.

Since there are so many of these incubators in operation around the country, chances are one is nearby. For more information and the location of the incubator nearest you, call the National Business Incubator Association at 740-593-4331 or the Small Business Administration at 1-800-827-5722.

Evaluating Your Skills

The following chart will help you identify your strengths and weaknesses, and will give you a better idea of whether you're ready to become a small business owner.

Examine each of the skills areas listed in the chart. Ask yourself whether you possess some or all of the skills listed. Then rate your skills in each area, using a scale of 1 to 5, with 1 meaning you have little skill in a particular area and 5 meaning you are very skilled.

Skills Self-Evaluation

Description of Needed Skills	Rating				
	1	2	3	4	5
Sales					
• Buying inventory or materials • Customer service follow-up • Sales planning • Managing a sales force • Negotiating • Tracking competitors • Direct selling to buyers					
Marketing					
• Advertising, promotion, PR • Developing marketing strategies • Annual marketing plans • Distribution channel planning • Media planning and buying • Product pricing • Writing advertising copy • Packaging design					
Financial Planning					
• Cash flow planning • Working with bankers • Evaluating financial data • Managing credit					
Accounting					
• Bookkeeping • Preparing monthly statements • Billing, payables, receivables • Handling payroll, sales and income taxes					
Administrative					
• Scheduling • Benefits administration • Handling payroll					
Personnel Management					
• Hiring • Motivating • Firing • General management skills					
Personal Business Skills					
• Oral presentation • Organizational skills • Written communication • Computer and word processing • Fax, e-mail experience					
Intangibles					
• Ability to work long and hard • Ability to deal with failure • Ability to manage risk and stress • Ability to work with and manage others • Ability to work alone • Family support					
Total					

After you've rated yourself in each area, total up the numbers:

- If your total is less than 20 points, you should reconsider whether owning a business is the right step for you.

- If your total is between 20 and 25, you're on the verge of being ready, but you may be wise to spend some time strengthening some of your weaker areas.

- If your total is above 25, you're ready to start a new business.

By completing this exercise, you've probably, in effect, made a list of what you like and don't like to do. Generally, we like doing things we're good at and we don't like doing things we're not good at. It's a simple approach, but it should help you start to focus.

Ultimately, when assessing your strengths, you need to consider: Are you good at what you want to do in your business? That might seem like a silly question, but you need to have a realistic view of your skills within the trade or business you hope to pursue. It's one thing to have the confidence you can succeed at whatever you try to do. It's quite another to actually have the skills that would justify your confidence. We're not here to second-guess you or question your abilities. But we do want to make it clear that you have to be honest with yourself.

If you've been an employee, you've probably received feedback, whether positive or negative, from employers or coworkers. You also may have a track record of promotions and increasing responsibility. These are the kinds of objective factors to consider in evaluating your capabilities.

Example

Recall John, our house painter who's thinking of starting his own painting business. Over the years, his responsibilities as an employee had expanded to include estimating the cost of jobs. In effect, he did everything the owner did, except negotiate with customers. This advancement seems to provide objective evidence John has developed the skills he needs to run his own business.

Common Responsibilities for Small Business Owners

If you're currently employed, you have first-hand knowledge of what it's like to be an employee. If you think going into business for yourself will mostly mean doing the same thing, but for yourself, you're in for a surprise. Small business owners are responsible for the entire business, which involves a lot more than just providing goods or services. It's likely that all the administrative and managerial duties currently performed by your employer will fall on you.

Sales taxes and payroll or self-employment taxes will have to be collected and paid. Accounts receivable and accounts payable will arise in almost any business setting. Customer service, keeping the appropriate equipment and supplies in stock, as well as tracking and maintaining inventory and work in progress are activities vital to most businesses. As a new small business owner, it's more than likely there'll be no one except you to do them. And you'll be doing these things *in addition to* the activities that directly relate to providing goods or services to your customers. Here's a rundown of common responsibilities small business owners must assume.

- **Tax collector** — If you sell goods at the retail level, you're responsible for collecting a sales tax for various government entities. If you have employees, you're responsible for collecting payroll taxes. And unlike an employee whose employer withholds and remits income tax, you'll be paying self-employment tax (or figuring withholding if your business is a separate entity, such as a corporation).

- **Manager/boss** — If you have employees, you'll be responsible for all of the human resources-related functions, including recruiting, hiring, training, firing and tracking benefits information. You'll be the one filling out all the insurance forms, answering employee questions and dealing with complaints. You'll have to make decisions about raises, workplace rules and time-off policies.

- **Sales/marketing/advertising executive** — In addition to planning your marketing and advertising campaigns, you'll have to carry them out. You may be called on to write advertising copy, do preliminary market research and visit prospective customers. Depending on the type of business you start, you may have to join business groups; attend various breakfasts, lunches and dinners; and just generally network with anyone who could help your business prosper.

- **Bookkeeper/accountant** — Even if you have an accountant, you'll have to know a lot about accounting; you'll have to know which records to keep and how to keep them. If you don't have an accountant, you'll also have to prepare all of your tax forms. And since current financial information is critical to success, you'll have to know how to prepare and interpret all of your own financial statements.

- **Lawyer** — Even if you have a lawyer, you'll have to know a lot about the law. If you don't have a lawyer, you'll have to prepare all of your own contracts (with suppliers, for example). If you hire employees, you'll need to understand and comply with federal and state employment laws.

- **Business planner** — Over time, you'll inevitably want or need to make changes. Perhaps you'll want to expand the business or add a new product line, or you may have to react to a new competitor. Whatever is required, you're the one who's going to have to make the crucial decisions, and then implement them. You won't be relieved of any of your other ongoing responsibilities, or get any extra time, when this occurs.

- **Bill collector** — When customers don't pay, it'll be up to you to collect from them. You'll have to know what you can and can't do when collecting, and you'll be the one who decides how best to collect from them and when to give up.

- **Market researcher** — Before you start your business, you'll have to find out who your customers are and where they're located; you may also have to conduct market research at various times during the life of your business, such as when you consider introducing a new product.

- **Technology expert** — As a small business owner, you'll probably come to depend upon your computer. You'll have to fix it when broken, install upgrades and load software; you'll also have to keep up with the newest products and the latest changes in technology.

- **Clerk/receptionist/typist/secretary** — Even if you have clerical help, you'll inevitably do some of your filing, some of your typing, some of your mailing and some of your telephone answering; even if you have someone else, for example, to keep track of overdue accounts, you'll have to know how to do it so you can teach them what to do.

We included this list of the important responsibilities of running a business so you can realistically appraise your chances for success. Obviously, much of your time will be spent on the mechanics of complying with the requirements imposed on you as a business owner. If you're going to succeed, you'll have to do so in the time that remains. Don't make the mistake of underestimating the cost, in hours, of being in business for yourself. A person who spends 40 hours a week focused on his or her work will have to work a lot more hours as a business owner to get in 40 hours of activity directly relating to providing customers goods or services. And during the startup period, you'll probably be the busiest you'll ever be.

CAN YOU HANDLE THE IMPACT ON YOUR LIFE?

Being self-employed is fundamentally different than being an employee. The distinction between work time and personal time blurs.

If a problem arises with the business, it's *your* problem, and it won't go away merely because you've closed the doors for the day. Decisions you make regarding the business will have a direct and immediate impact on your personal life. For example, if you're in retail and decide to remain open evenings, it's your time that's affected. And you're likely to be on call 24 hours a day in the event an emergency arises regarding your business.

The impact is even greater if your business involves working out of your home. You may experience conflicts over the use of space for business or personal purposes. The distinction between your personal life and business life is even further attenuated. Even when you're at home, you're also physically at work. On the upside, there's no commute and you can eat cheaper at home.

If you have a family, it's important to measure the impact opening a new business will have on them. It's best to discuss this as soon as you seriously start to consider the idea. Both you and your family must be willing to put up with the changes in your lives owning a business will bring. Some people experience emotional and physical strain from being on their own and working the hours it takes to make it.

Certainty of Source and Amount of Income

One of the biggest differences between being self-employed and being an employee is the source of your income. Employees can generally expect to receive a paycheck at fixed intervals and for a known amount. (Those working on commission or receiving tips have less certainty regarding the amount.) As the owner of a new small business, you'll be paid only when and if the business generates enough money. Even successful businesses rarely generate a profit in the beginning stages of operation. You'll have to be prepared for a period during which your expenses will exceed any income derived from the new business.

Health Insurance and Retirement Saving

Although employees are being called upon to pay an increasingly larger share of health insurance costs, it's even tougher for a small business owner. There is no employer to pick up some portion of the premium cost. There's no pool of employees that would allow you to negotiate a more favorable rate than you can get on an individual policy. On the other hand, you may be able to join an association of other small businesses so you can take advantage of cheaper group insurance rates.

For those covered under employer-provided health care plans who leave to start a business, there's the option of continuing coverage through the former employer's plan under the COBRA law. However, you're responsible for the full cost of premiums: The former employer generally won't be contributing anything for you. Also, you're entitled to continued coverage for a limited period of time: as little as 18 months or as long as 36 months, depending on the circumstances. You might be able to get better coverage for the same cost elsewhere. If your spouse has insurance through an employer plan, consider coverage through that plan.

Retirement savings are a little different than health insurance. If you don't have health insurance and experience a catastrophic injury or disease, you may be wiped out. The impact of failing to save for your retirement can be even more damaging, but people tend to minimize the risk because "retirement is such a long way off." It's no surprise the saving rate is higher among employees than small business owners. Employer-sponsored plans provide a convenient and painless way to set aside a portion of each paycheck. A small business owner has to make a conscious decision to save, outside the framework of a plan administered by someone else. That decision often can be deferred or forgotten when you feel the cash coming in has to be put right back into the business.

Chapter 2

The Right Small Business For You

The analysis you performed while reading the preceding chapter should have established that you're willing to make the commitment to open a business and you have many of the skills needed to make a go of it. As noted, many small businesses are, in fact, spin-offs of other businesses, such as the house painter who wants to start his own painting business. However, many people are looking for a change, and the last thing they want is to open businesses like the ones where they're employed.

Whether you've already got a solid idea of what business to open or you're seriously undecided, you need to assess the specific types of businesses you're interested in from a number of perspectives. In this chapter, we'll look at the steps you should take in selecting a business.

- Perform the market research necessary to determine:

  — what types of businesses have the potential to succeed in the area in which you wish to locate, and

  — if there are enough potential customers to make it economically viable to start the type of business you want.

- Assess how well your skills match those required by the businesses you're considering. Determine if it's reasonable to acquire additional expertise, through employment or education, to bring your skill set in line with the demands of the business.

- Look at the mistakes others have made in the business selection process in order to learn what doesn't work.

CHOOSING A TYPE OF BUSINESS

Most books on the subject of selecting a small business will tell you to start by matching your skills and experience to some business that requires those skills. For example, if you love to cook, they'll suggest you open a catering business or a restaurant. Considering doing something you love is a start, but it has to be further analyzed by examining the market potential, competition, resources required to enter the market, consumer/buyer demand and uniqueness of the idea.

Work Smart

The best place to start in picking a small business is with consumers (including other businesses that may want your product or service). What do consumers or businesses want that's not being provided to them? Ultimately, whether you succeed will depend upon whether you're able to meet some unmet need in the market.

In fact, regardless of what you like to do, you'll have to select a business that meets an unfilled need. Let's assume the community in which you want to locate your business has more than enough caterers to serve the population, but not nearly enough interior decorators. You're far more likely to succeed if you attempt to address the unmet need for interior decorators rather than to enter the already-crowded catering market. Unless your heart is set on food preparation, it pays to go where there are potential customers looking to spend their money. You can always hire people with decorating skills, or develop them on your own through training, education, or by trial and error. It's far easier to acquire skills or hire someone than it is to sell consumers something they don't need or want.

Of course, you don't necessarily have to sell a new or different product or service in order to succeed; you can succeed if you can improve what is already being sold. In the above example, you should open a catering business if you can provide a better service than other catering businesses, such as a wider menu or lower prices. But that's *still* a function of what consumers want. Proper research would have told you there is a demand for a new catering business if prices were lower or if the menu were more varied.

IS THERE A MARKET FOR YOUR BUSINESS?

Market research is arguably the most important element in making a decision to open a new business. The purpose of market research is to determine whether you can reasonably expect a business of the type you've chosen to succeed in a particular market. The more information you have, the better you'll be able to answer the key questions about the potential success of your business idea:

- What are conditions like in general for this type of business? You need to do an industry analysis as well as an assessment of the general environment in which you plan to compete.

  — Does the industry have adequate supplies of materials or labor? Is technology changing rapidly? Is government regulation a concern?

  — How will the overall economic outlook, and the outlook in your area, affect your new business? Is the local population growing? What are income levels doing? Will these trends help or hurt your new business?

- Who will be your customers? A target market analysis identifies and quantifies the customers you will try to serve.

  — Will your customers be the ultimate consumers or will you sell your products or services through a distributor, wholesaler or other reseller?

  — What are the characteristics of your prospective customers, and how will they help or hurt your chances for success?

- Who will you be competing against? A competitive analysis identifies your competitors and potential competitors, examining their strengths and weaknesses.

  — How big is the competition, and what type of financial resources will they have available?

  — Are competitors gaining or losing market share in the market you wish to enter?

  — Are competitors actively seeking to grow through new product and service offerings?

- How will your business stack up? A needs analysis describes your perceptions regarding the met and unmet needs of your target market.

  — What needs are currently being met, and how can you improve upon delivery to break down already-established customer loyalty?

  — What needs are unmet, and are there good reasons for it?

  — Are trends emerging that will affect how you serve your target market?

Industry Analysis

Unless you've come up with a completely new and unique idea for a product or service that never existed before, there are already existing businesses similar to what you're considering. The existence of these businesses is helpful, since it means several types of organizations have probably already compiled information important to your analysis. While not true of every type of business, you can get information about most industries through:

- **Publications** — Industry organizations or trade associations often publish and maintain industry-specific information and on-line databases.

- **Government entities** — State and local government agencies, including the Census Bureau and state commerce departments, record the flow of trade.

- **Regional membership groups** — Local organizations and trade associations may provide details because membership is limited to businesses located in a specific geographic region.

- **Industry experts** — Certain sources research and offer data and analysts' opinions about the largest players in an industry (e.g., Standard & Poor's reports, quotes from reputable news sources).

What types of information will these sources provide? Here's several types of data that will help you to evaluate your business idea:

- **Statistics about the size of the industry** — How many businesses are there in this industry, and what were the industry's overall sales figures for last year? Is the industry expanding, contracting or holding steady?

- **The industry's major participants** — While you may or may not compete directly against these companies (they are likely to be large, national or international corporations), it's important to identify them and have a good understanding of their market share, and why they are or aren't successful.

- **Important trends affecting the industry** — You should also try to learn about these. For example, significant changes in the target market, technology or in other related industries may affect the prospects for your particular business.

The *Directory of On-Line Resources* and the *Data Base Catalog* are popular books listing many resources available over your computer modem. Or if your prefer to do research the old-fashioned (print-based) way, look up a book called *Knowing Where to Look: The Ultimate Guide to Research* by Louis Horowitz, published by Writer's Digest. The American Marketing Association (the "other" AMA) may be able to help you as well. Visit their web site at www.marketingpower.com or call them at 1-800-262-1150.

Target Market Analysis

How do you determine if there are enough people in your market willing to purchase what you have to offer, at the price you need to charge to make a profit? The best way is to conduct a methodical analysis of the market you plan to reach. The objective is to know who your customers will be and whether there are enough potential customers to support your business.

The first step is to look at the factors that will define your market:

- **Geographic scope** — A mail-order house can reasonably target people located throughout the entire country and beyond. In contrast, a landscape service is likely to provide services within a relatively limited geographic area.

- **Demographics** — These are tangible, measurable facts that distinguish one group of people from another. No matter who you're targeting for the selling of goods or services, you need to know as much about them as you possibly can. Family income, education level, occupations, family makeup and size, and other factors may all be used to describe your target market.

Example

When you think about your potential market, remember that it can be defined by a number of different characteristics. For example, a coffee and donut shop has a market that is geographically limited. Only those who are in the neighborhood will eat there. Similarly, a jewelry store specializing in expensive, high-end items has a market that's limited to the number of potential customers with sufficient financial resources. A dive shop's market is limited to those who have an interest in diving, swimming or snorkeling.

- **Lifestyle** — This analysis is more concerned with intangibles. Many businesses serve markets defined by choices made with respect to lifestyle. Your target market may well be defined, at least in part, by peoples' hobbies, recreational and entertainment preferences, ethnic or religious practices, or political beliefs.

- **Other buyers' characteristics** — If you plan to sell to other businesses, which will resell your products and services, your buyers are predominantly channel buyers. Typical channel buyers include local, regional and national distributors; wholesalers; and retail or chain store buyers. Influences on channel buyers may include attributes such as the item's margin and profitability, discounts, free goods, cash fees and personal relationships.

- **Size** — Are there enough potential customers in your target market to generate the amount of revenue needed to consider your new business a success? To some extent, you'll be able to estimate whether the market is large enough based on the other information you collect.

Fortunately, a lot of this information is readily available in many areas of the country. City and county governments collect, compile and publish this information. Real estate sales companies make use of this material to tout the benefits of the areas in which they sell. Local libraries also keep this information on file.

If you have a particular geographic location in mind, go there and spend some time looking at the community. You can tell a lot about an area just by the way it looks, the types of cars you see parked, and how well maintained it is. Vacant, run-down housing says much about a community. A college or university town differs from a similar town with no school.

Example

Consider John, our prospective house painter from Chapter 1. Let's assume he doesn't want to open up in direct competition with his former employer, for a variety of reasons. Chief among them is the fact John lives over 50 miles from the community in which he currently works as an employee, and he'd like to work closer to home.

Upon examining the geographic market in which he'd like to work, John discovers there's a lot of new construction going on, but not much renovation work. Based on this, John may change his target market from homeowners wanting their houses painted to general contractors wanting new homes painted.

The more characteristics of your prospective customers you can identify, the more easily you can pinpoint the purchasing patterns and trends your business must capitalize on or accommodate in order to be successful. If you expect to have several types of customers (e.g., you plan to sell at both retail and wholesale), you'll want to describe separately the important characteristics of each group.

Once obtained, this information can help you in two very important ways. It can help you develop your product or service to better match what your customers are likely to want. It can also tell you how to reach your customers through advertising, promotions, etc.

Competitive Analysis

Having defined the characteristics of the market you'd like to reach, the next step is to focus on those businesses that will be in direct competition with yours. By identifying competitors early on, you reduce the risk of wasting valuable time and resources investigating an idea that won't pan out. If the competition is strong and well-entrenched, it may be difficult for you, as a newcomer, to enter the market at all. The following classification scheme can help you assess how much of a challenge a particular competitor will present.

- **First-level competitors** — These are the specific businesses or products directly competing with you in your geographic area. In many cases, these competitors offer a product or service interchangeable with yours in the eyes of consumers (although, of course, you hope you hold the advantage with better quality, more convenient distribution and other special features).

Example

First-level competition for a lawn and garden center would be other lawn and garden centers directly competing for and serving the same geographic area.

- **Second-level competitors** — These businesses offer similar products in a different business category or are more remote geographically. None of these competitors provides exactly the same mix of products and services as you, but each may be picking off some of the most lucrative parts of your business.

Example

Second-level competitors of a lawn and garden center would be a discount chain selling garden supplies and plants in season, a landscaping contractor who will provide and install the plants, and a mail-order house selling garden tools and plants in seed or bulb form.

- **Third-level competitors** — These businesses compete for the "same-occasion" dollars.

Example

Because gardening is a hobby for some people, third-level competitors might include businesses providing other types of entertainment or hobby equipment. Because gardening can also be considered a type of home improvement, competitors might be providers of other home-improvement supplies and services.

The aim of this analysis is to consider carefully, from your prospective customers' viewpoint, all available alternatives to purchasing from you. Knowing that, you can try to make sure your business provides advantages over your competitors, beginning with those most directly similar to you. In fact, you can even borrow ideas from second- or third-level competitors so as to compete more effectively against the first tier.

Competitors' Strengths and Weaknesses

It's to your advantage to know as much as you reasonably can about the identity of your competitors and the details of your competitors' businesses. Study their ads, brochures and promotional materials. Drive past their location (and if it's a retail business, make some purchases there, incognito if necessary). Talk to their customers and examine their pricing. What are they doing well that you can copy, and what are they doing poorly that you can capitalize on?

Moreover, you may need to know a wealth of other facts, depending on the type of business you have. For example, if you're considering catalog sales, you'll want to know how fast your competitors can fulfill a typical order, what they charge for shipping and handling, etc.

Company data from competitors may be available by interviewing competitor company executives, attending industry trade shows and asking the right questions from industry experts. They may be unaffordable as consultants, but willing to direct you to free databases you would not ordinarily know of or have access to. And don't overlook your competitors' suppliers. They can be excellent sources of information to aid your research.

Future Competition

Along with your current competitors, give some thought to the possibility that other competition will arise in the near future. Unfortunately, if you're successful, you'll be encouraging others to start businesses to serve the same customers. Consider what barriers there would be for others starting a new business in your industry and market. Is it relatively easy, or relatively difficult, to join the fray in terms of capital, staffing, inventory, distribution control, work force, relationships with suppliers, etc.? Since your business is new, you'll have to think about how you can overcome these hurdles yourself.

Needs Analysis

Remember, while you may be drawn to a particular type of business because of your knowledge of its operations, or your affinity with the type of product or service you're planning to offer, ultimately, your success will depend on how well you satisfy your customers' needs.

A small business operating an auto repair shop must remember that customers patronize the shop because they need reliable transportation. Everything the shop does must come together to serve that need. By focusing on the customers' needs, the shop owner can devise ways to improve service in the eyes of the customers, *such as by offering loaner cars, providing free rides to the customers' workplace or guaranteeing the service performed for a specified period. The typical auto shop customer is less likely to be concerned about the decor of the shop or about bargain-basement prices, since those don't immediately impact on the need for transportation.*

Once you've come up with what you believe to be the customers' most important needs in relation to your products or services, and to your category of business in general, you can divide your list into two parts: needs already being met successfully in the marketplace and needs remaining unfilled. You can then describe the ways in which your business will fill these gaps in the marketplace.

You have to be aware of the needs already being filled, so you can avoid being simply a "me-too" business with little chance of breaking down your customers' already-established loyalty to another provider. Particularly if the competition is well-established with a substantial market share, it will be difficult to break in unless you do a noticeably better job of meeting more of your customers' needs.

On the other hand, very few customer needs go unnoticed and unserved for long. If you believe you've discovered a huge, gaping hole in the marketplace, chances are the need isn't as large as it appears, the need can't be profitably satisfied, or competitors are already making plans to move into the market.

Although there are a few exceptions, particularly where new technology is being employed, most small businesses can thrive by becoming more closely attuned to their customers' needs, and offering a product or service combination that meets those needs in a significantly superior way.

You may discover virtually all of the customer's needs are already being filled. If so, you'll have to reexamine the situation a bit. Either you must dig deeper to uncover more unmet needs or dramatically rethink your business plan. Perhaps going into a slightly different type of business would allow you to function in a marketplace that's not quite as saturated.

If money is not an issue, you may want to contact a market research firm, ask them to analyze your community and find out where small business opportunities exist. If, like for most of us, money is an issue, you'll have to gather all or most of the information yourself.

A good place to start is with the mainstream press: your local newspaper, *The New York Times*, *The Wall Street Journal*, *Time, U.S. News and World Report* and *Newsweek*. You also should look at the business press: *Fortune, Forbes, Business Week* or any of the other business periodicals available. When reading them, look for trends that may be emerging, not just in business but in our culture at large.

In addition to reading newspapers and magazines, you should talk to friends, relatives, business associates and other small business owners about ideas they may have or needs in the market they don't believe are being met. And last but not least, don't forget the often most-overlooked resource—yourself. You're a consumer. If you've wished a particular service were available, chances are others have too.

Also, when you ponder market opportunities, think about how you can improve upon a product or service already being provided. But be aware of at least two potential stumbling blocks here. First, there is the tendency to believe too readily that you can improve upon an existing product or service. This is just old-fashioned overconfidence. Be sure you've thought through the specific steps you can take to improve what's already out there. Second, being able to improve upon a product or service is no guarantee of its success. In other words, you also must be sure there is a demand for the improvement.

Niche Marketing

An approach perhaps even more effective than tackling existing businesses head-on is to look for ways you can perform a service or provide a product similar to, but not quite the same as, a service or product already being provided. One example of this approach is to look for a special niche within a given field.

Example

 Betsy used to have a job as an accountant in a large accounting firm. Occasionally, her duties included work for film companies that came to town for a shoot.

Betsy did a little research and found there weren't any other accountants who specifically served the needs of the film market. She also found out there were enough film companies that came to town each year for her to make a nice living serving only them.

Betsy quit and started her own firm, specializing in accounting for the film industry.

To develop a niche, you should be looking for anomalies in the market. In marketing terms, an anomaly is an unmet need whose time has come to be filled. To support a profitable business, the need must be fairly widespread or rapidly growing.

Although people wanted to be able to send letters and packages overnight anywhere in the country, they didn't think it was possible. Enter Federal Express and—presto—a $500 million startup business serving an anomaly.

Where are today's anomalies? Perhaps one lies hidden in the social and business trends now underway. For example, a lot of couples with both partners working would like hot, delivered, home-cooked meals that vary each night. This situation could present an interesting possibility.

Consider Social Trends

One great way to find market opportunities for your product or service is to study social and business trends. The challenge for you will be to see if you can find business opportunities in any of these trends:

- **Baby boomers entering their 50s** — This group has the largest amount of disposable income in history! They're driving growth in many areas, including services, recreation and general retailing. Consider what that means for opportunities in travel, recreation, vacations, entertainment, food and clothing.

- **New boomer crop of children** — While the original boomers had fewer children per household than their parents, their children seem to be having more, thus creating a new crop of boomer grandchildren in the near future. Consider what that means for opportunities in child care, toys and clothing.

- **Growing disparity between rich and poor** — The middle class is shrinking. Consider what that means for opportunities in home ownership, cars, entertainment and restaurants.

- **Increasing globalization of business** — This should, if anything, continue to accelerate in the coming years. Consider what that means for opportunities in emerging world markets, particularly in China, the old Soviet Union and Southeast Asia.

- **Reinvention of religion** — As people continue to cast off traditional beliefs and services, others return to them even more vigorously. Consider what that means for opportunities in books, tapes and online services.

- **Yearning for high-touch products and services** — This includes the nostalgia induced by high-tech solutions to everything. Consider what that means for opportunities in antiques, older homes, home delivery and pickup businesses, and any business owned by friendly service-minded proprietors.

- **Mass customization** — This is not an oxymoron, but a response to global homogeneity. Consider what that means for opportunities in businesses providing products or services individually tailored to each customer.

MATCHING SKILLS TO BUSINESSES

Presumably, at this point, you've already identified some need in the market that is not being met. If so, you're ready to match your skills with those unmet needs, with the goal of finding the right small business for you. If not, you may want to review our discussion on assessing the needs of your particular target market.

To find a good match, you should begin by listing what you enjoy doing, what your hobbies are, which skills you've acquired, what your work experiences have been, and what your goals are for the business. The following chart is designed to help you make the right decision, based on your unique set of circumstances.

Business Selection Chart

IDEA					
Knowledge					
Experience					
Skills					
Ease of entry					
Uniqueness					
TOTAL					

To fill it out, follow these three steps:

(1) In the top row, labeled "Idea," list the business ideas you're considering by order of interest. So in the left-most blank space, put the idea you're most interested in. Enter the next most-favorable idea in the next space and so forth, until you've listed all of your possible ideas across the top of the chart.

(2) Now take each idea and rate it on a scale of 0 to 3 in each of the categories listed. Use the following rating system: 0—none; 1—below average; 2—average; and 3—above average.

Here's a look at each of the categories and some of the things you should consider when rating them:

- **Your knowledge of the business** — How much do you know about the field? Will you have to spend extra time and money teaching yourself the business? Will you have to take on a partner because you don't know the business well enough? *Rating:* 0—no knowledge of the business; 1—some indirect knowledge of the business; 2—limited knowledge; 3—working knowledge.

- **Your experience in the field** — In some cases, you may have a lot of knowledge about the subject, but not much experience. Have you ever owned or worked in this type of business before? To what extent is hands-on experience crucial to the business? *Rating:* 0—no experience; 1—indirect experience; 2—limited experience; 3—familiarity with the business.

- **Your skills** — For now, ignore those skills that might be common to each of your ideas, and try to concentrate on skills that are unique to that business. To what extent do you possess those skills? If you lack them, how difficult will it be to acquire them? *Rating:* 0—none; 1—limited skills; 2—some skills; 3—extensive skills.

- **Ease of entry** — Think both of the costs of entering the business and of the competitive barriers that might exist. For example, a service business you can run from your home might be relatively inexpensive to start, but if several others are already providing that service, entry in the field may be difficult. *Rating:* 0—crowded field, very difficult to enter; 1—limited entry available; 2—mix of large and small competitors; 3—virtually unrestricted entry for any size business.

- **Uniqueness** — This does not necessarily mean literally no one else is providing the same product or service; it can mean no one else is providing the product or service in the same way you intend to provide it, or it can mean no one else is providing that product or service in your area. Remember, you're looking for some way to distinguish your product or service from others who are already in business. *Rating:* 0—your product or service is widely available; 1—there are a few to several others offering your product or service; 2—there are only one or two others; 3—there are no others providing your product or service.

(3) Now total up the numbers. Here are some tips for making sense of the numbers and for narrowing your list of possible business choices:

- eliminate any idea not scoring a total of 10 or more

- eliminate any idea not scoring at least a 2 in almost every category

How many ideas are left? If the answer is "none," then you should use the list to identify where you need to improve so you can develop a strategy for raising the 1s to 2s or 3s. If the answer is "more than one," you have a pleasant dilemma: a choice of which business to start. If the answer is "one," you just may have found the perfect business for you.

Although making such a list might seem at first to be a little simplistic, you'll be surprised at how much writing down your ideas will help you crystallize what you want from a small business.

Now, compare the list you've just made with your list of what the market wants. Do any obvious matches leap out at you? If not, don't give up. Here are some more suggestions for choosing a new business:

- **Find something you like** — Look at the list compiled from your market research; eliminate any business you don't believe you'll *really* enjoy owning. As a small business owner, you'll be living, sleeping and breathing your business. If you don't enjoy that business, your chances for success are slim.

- **Be realistic** — On the other hand, be wary of relying too heavily on your list of interests when making your choice. Don't forget: Much of a small business owner's time is spent on tasks such as managing employees, haggling with suppliers, meeting with your lawyer or accountant, etc.

- **Consider the cost** — If you don't have a lot of money to start with, look for a business where you get paid up front and don't have a lot of startup costs.

Example

 Suppose you love photography. If you open a store that sells photographic equipment, you'll have to rent space, purchase inventory for the store and probably extend credit to customers. That'll cost you a lot up front, and you won't see any money coming in until your customers pay you.

The results would be about the same if you opened a film processing and printing business. You'll have to pay rent, purchase equipment and supplies, and wait for customers to drop off their film for developing.

On the other hand, if you offer your services as a freelance photographer, you probably can operate this business from home and should get paid (at least in part) at the time of the shoot.

- **Choose a growth opportunity** — Look for businesses where you'll have a lot of repeat customers or where people will need to keep buying supplies from you.

- **Understand the cycle of business** — Avoid seasonal businesses (however, if you're willing and able to ride out the slow months, these businesses—such as beachwear shops, ski shops, farm produce, Christmas-related stores and services, and anything to do with schools and colleges—can provide you with a lot of time off).

- **Know the competition** — Avoid going head-to-head with discounters or with well-established businesses, since it will be just about impossible to compete with their prices. Instead, you'll have to compete in service.

- **Balance your startup plans and goals** — Service businesses are the easiest and cheapest to start because you don't have to buy a lot of equipment and might not need any employees, at least at first (although if your goal is someday to sell the business and retire, you should be aware these businesses are also often the hardest to sell because the primary asset is usually you).

CHOOSING A BUSINESS: COMMON MISTAKES

Although there are many reasons why small businesses fail, one of the most common mistakes occurs when choosing a small business. A lot of people simply make the wrong choice. To help you avoid that error, here's a look at four of the top reasons why wrong choices are made.

Error #1: Overestimating demand — Don't convert a hobby or interest into a small business without first finding out if there is sufficient demand for the product or service to be provided.

Error #2: Starting the business without adequate planning — Your success is not guaranteed just because you've found a market opportunity that also takes advantage of your skills and experience. There are many other considerations. For example, you still have to figure out if you can raise enough money to get started and withstand periods in which little or no revenue is coming in.

Error #3: Resisting the urge to ask for help — Since you're reading this material, you already may have avoided this pitfall. However, a lot of people are reluctant to ask others for advice in choosing a business, either because they are too proud or don't know help is available. Help is out there, and if you shop wisely, it won't cost you an arm and leg to get it.

- **Talk to others operating the same or similar businesses** — You may be surprised at how many small business owners will be willing to share their insights with you. Provided you're not asking for trade secrets—and especially if you won't be a direct competitor—you may pick up some valuable information. The local Chamber of Commerce or other business association meetings may provide access to business owners you can talk to. If you don't make any headway by attending such meetings or directly approaching business owners, you may wish to offer a consulting fee. This may seem like a dubious expense, since you're not yet open for business. But if you are able to find out what you need to know about the day-to-day operation of your prospective business, this one-time expense will probably be money well spent.

- **Work for someone else for a while** — A time-honored way of learning a business is to work in a similar business as an employee. Not only will you be getting on-the-job training, but you'll be getting a paycheck and avoiding overhead expenses. When scouting potential employer-trainers, it's best to look for one that is successful and well run. Even though you may be able to learn as much about your particular business from a poorly run, inefficient operation—the idea being, "see their mistakes and don't repeat them"—this can be frustrating and time-consuming. Although there may be a few different ways to do any job successfully, there are probably a thousand ways to mess it up! You don't need to learn all these mistakes in order to figure out the secrets to success.

Error #4: Trying to start a business with too little money — Much of the focus of this chapter has been on what you want to do. That makes sense because you certainly aren't going to be happy if you choose a business that involves doing work you don't like. But after you have a handle on what you want to do, the following questions must be answered: How much will it cost, and where will you get the money? An under-funded startup business is highly likely to wind up as a failed business.

Chapter 3

Can You Afford To Go Into Business?

Previously, we touched on some of the personal financial factors that merit attention in deciding if you want to start a new business. Unless you're launching a part-time business, you'll probably be giving up some or all of your current income in order to start the business. This may limit the amount of money you can spend out of your own pocket on the expenses associated with starting your new business.

This chapter will take you, step-by-step, through some financial analysis that should make it clear, one way or the other, whether or not you can afford to go into business for yourself. This is a general inquiry: that is, it's not intended to provide the precise dollar figure you can expect to spend starting your particular business. Instead, the focus is on your personal and family economic needs, sources of income, and availability of money to start a business.

Once individual and family finances have been analyzed, it's time to examine sources of startup funding for your business, above and beyond what you personally can afford to dedicate to the venture. Depending on the scope of your business, you may need to borrow some money to cover the balance of the cost of starting and running your new operation.

In the following chapters, we'll explore how the specific decisions you make about your business's organization, location, facilities and numerous other factors affect the actual dollar amount you'll need. But for now, let's begin with a snapshot of your current financial condition.

ANALYZING YOUR PERSONAL FINANCES

Before you start planning for the cash needs of your new business, you must determine how much money you will need to survive. You have to plan for personal cash needs during the startup and first few months of your new venture. It would be nice to think your business will be profitable from the day you open the doors, but that's not realistic.

In Chapter 1, we discussed how to quantify your goals and suggested a good exercise would be to look at your current financial situation. Now let's take it one step further. The best way to start is to prepare a family budget schedule showing how you will spend your money in the next 12 months.

It is advisable to use a monthly schedule because expenses may fluctuate greatly from month to month. For example, if you have children in private school or college, and the tuition is due twice a year, then those months will require additional cash. Be sure to include all of your expenses, ranging from home mortgage payments to vacations to doctor bills. When preparing the schedule, also keep in mind the expenses that could be reduced or eliminated, if needed.

For those of you who have already established a family budget, there may not be much to this exercise. For the rest of us, it's a critical component of the planning process. You need to know exactly what it costs you to live, because any business that can't eventually meet your current economic needs isn't worth starting.

Of course, you may be happy making less than you do now, at least at first, just to be your own boss. Conversely, you may be sliding into debt, and you know you need to earn more than you currently make. Either way, an assessment of the source of your money, and how it's used, is necessary to establish the affordability of your new business.

Family Monthly Budget

The following worksheet summarizes your income for the coming year, from all sources other than your new business, on a month-by-month basis. Don't omit anything. If your mother sends you a check every year on your birthday, include it. We're not looking at taxable income here, just the actual amount of money you have available each month to spend.

While going through your monthly analysis, you will probably find that in some months you will have extra cash, while in others you will be short of funds. If the months you are short are the result of some extra expense, like a long vacation, you need to determine your cash priorities. If every year you think you need to spend that money on a vacation, then include it in your budget. Also, you may want to factor in an additional 5 to 10 percent of total costs for unexpected expenses, just to be safe. Finally, you need to plan for emergencies, like a major repair on the car. These costs will not be part of your budget, but you should always have an emergency fund set aside for these types of expenses.

Your particular expenses may not match your income, on a month-by-month basis, but total annual expenses should equal total annual income. If expenses exceed income, then you'll be going further and further into debt. Getting that situation under control should probably be a higher priority than starting a business.

In the course of putting together a budget, you may decide to make changes in how you spend your money. For example, you may decide to spend less on entertainment or to forego saving any money during the startup period of your business. The bottom line is this: How much do you need just to get by? The answer to that question is the minimum economic goal you can set for a small business. No matter how appealing a business idea may be, if your best forecast only brings ever-increasing personal debt with no turnaround in sight, you shouldn't start the business at all.

Work Smart

To better your chances of affording a new business, you will want to make monetary preparations well in advance. Start saving now for the inevitable lean times that will come during the startup phase. Make some discretionary cuts in spending, sooner rather than later. You'll save money now and possibly lower future budgetary expenses. Don't wait until you're ready to open the business to make changes in your family finances.

Note that this discussion assumes you'll be giving up your current source of income in order to start your business. Many people start a business in their spare time or have a spouse who's going to continue to earn money elsewhere, even after the new business is up and running. Be sure to account for these funds in your calculations. If it costs you $40,000 a year to live, and you anticipate $25,000 in income from other sources, your new business will only have to generate $15,000 to keep your finances in balance. Whatever you do, be realistic, both about what you really need and what you can expect your business to generate.

After you have determined what income you will need to support yourself and family during the development of your new business, what comes next? How long are you willing to go with a loss in your new business? How long are you willing to be just scraping by and

Family Monthly Budget Schedule					
	JAN	**FEB**	**MAR**	**APR**	**MAY**
Income Description:					
Wages (take-home) partner 1					
Wages (take-home) partner 2					
Interest and dividends					
Other					
Total Income					
Expense Description:					
Auto expense					
Auto insurance					
Auto payment					
Beauty shop and barber					
Cable TV					
Charity					
Child care					
Clothing					
Credit card payments					
Dues and subscriptions					
Entertainment and recreation					
Gifts					
Groceries and outside meals					
Health insurance					
Home repairs					
Household					
Income tax (additional)					
Laundry and dry cleaning					
Life insurance					
Medical and dental					
Mortgage payment or rent					
Other debt payments					
Telephone bill					
Tuition					
Utilities					
Vacations					
Other					
Total Expenses					
Cash (Shortfall) Extra					

Family Monthly Budget Schedule							
JUN	JUL	AUG	SEP	OCT	NOV	DEC	TOTAL

have only enough to pay the business expenses? Finally, how much income do you want to make in your new business? At this point, you should have the goal in mind (and written down) that can answer these questions.

Potential new business owners should consider a one- to three-year plan for family survival, at a minimum. Lack of staying power, especially in small businesses that may not generate enough cash to live on for a year or two, is one of the reasons small businesses fail.

ANALYZING YOUR STARTUP EXPENSES

One of the most common reasons small businesses fail is that the owners underestimate how much money they will need to start the new venture. It always seems to cost more than they thought. Have you ever heard the old adage about planning a trip from the U.S. to Europe: Plan what you should wear and how much it will cost, then halve the clothes and double the money. Perhaps we need a similar adage about starting a small business.

The lesson to be learned from the many small business failures is you need to be extremely careful when determining how much money is necessary to start your new business. Don't fall into the "rosy forecast" trap in which the new owner over-optimistically predicts robust sales in the first year and, as a result, doesn't have enough money on hand when the cash flow dries up.

An Opening Estimate

The first time you go through the costs to start a new business, you do not need to be particularly precise. You can just "ballpark" the amount to get a rough idea of your expected startup costs. Later, in Chapter 10, we'll go into more detail regarding the actual costs involved.

For now, you just need to consider the scope of your particular business and what it means in terms of the following categories:

- **Professional assistance** — You'll need to pay for the help of a lawyer, accountant and perhaps other professionals, such as a marketing or business consultant (for more details, see Chapter 4.)

- **Insurance** — Whatever type of business you launch, you'll want to protect it and your personal assets. Your particular needs will depend on the scope of your operation (for more details, see Chapter 4).

- **Advertising and marketing** — Every new business has unique needs in this area. The amount you'll have to spend depends upon the industry you're in and the competition you'll have, as well as your personal philosophy (for more details, see Chapter 7).

- **Employees** — If you have staffing needs, there are a number of ancillary costs associated with hiring help. Besides payroll, there are benefits, tax and compliance issues (for more details, see Chapter 9).

- **Physical space** — Whether small office or home office, this has the potential to be your biggest cash outlay. This includes not only the cost of the location, but equipping it as well (for more details, see Chapter 8).

- **Special retail considerations** — Storefront operations have certain costs that other types of operations won't have: cash for the register, beginning inventory, and construction and decorating expenses (for more details, see Chapter 10).

- **Miscellaneous** — Besides licenses, permits and utility deposits, there will be a series of unanticipated expenses, and many of these costs are business-specific. A good rule of thumb is 10 percent of the total estimate.

- **Raising money** — It costs money to borrow money, and any interest or fees must go into your opening budget.

Work Smart

As you work through these topics, don't forget that your accountant can be a great source of information for helping you make startup cost estimates. If your accountant has small business experience, he or she should be able to tell you whether your estimates are on target.

Remember to think of these costs in terms of the initial startup period as well as for the first 90 days you're open for business. Your estimate must get you through the inevitable lean times that will come during the early months of operation. So don't underestimate this figure. It's better to err on the high side. After all, you're just looking for a round number to use for your affordability calculations. Actual costs will be determined later, as you get closer to opening.

Raising Your Investment Cash

Once the estimate is done, you can begin to consider the amount of money needed to open your business, with the objective of determining whether you'll need to borrow some portion of it. Don't forget, though, any interest payment becomes part of the overall estimate you'll need.

If you believe you already have enough money for startup, you've cleared a major hurdle. Usually, most small businesses won't be able to get a bank loan for opening costs. Banks are conservative lenders and require a proven track record before approving loan money.

If the opening estimate is greater than your available resources, you'll have to find other sources of money. But to raise that cash, you'll probably have to demonstrate your willingness to invest in the venture as well. Without a large personal investment, you'll have a hard time convincing others to back the business.

Sources of Funding

By most estimates, you'll have to fund the majority, if not all, of the initial startup costs for your new business. Let's take a look at some of the ways you might raise the money:

- **Personal savings** — If you have the money in savings and don't need to raise it elsewhere, that's great. But be careful about using your retirement savings to fund a new business. There is always a risk in starting a new business, so make sure to evaluate your alternatives carefully. In fact, unless you have cash over and above what you intend to use as a retirement fund, you probably should raise the money elsewhere.

- **Friends and family** — If you don't have the money on hand, friends and family are normally the least expensive way to raise funds because they may not charge you interest, they won't require you to submit a business plan, and they're usually the only ones who will fall for your pleas for sympathy. (Try the "I don't have any collateral or business experience but I *really* need the money" approach on your banker and see if it works. If it does, please send us the name and address of our new banker.)

- **Partnerships** — Another means of raising startup money is to bring in a partner who has the funds. But use caution when taking on a partner. Remember, you will have to give up something in return for the money, usually some of the control, profit and freedom of running your own business. (For more information on setting up a partnership, see Chapter 6.)

- **Other equity money** — Equity money can come in the form of private investments from friends, family and interested strangers. The interested strangers may be other successful companies that wish to have an interest in your company. And they may bring the same kind of expertise and industry experience to the table.

Work Smart

If you borrow money from your family or friends, put it in writing and treat it like it any other loan. If they don't ask you to pay interest, then set up the loan to pay them whatever the prime rate is.

Although this will protect them, you're doing it to protect yourself as well. Suppose your uncle decides to take an expensive vacation and wants his money back? The document should spell out under which conditions the money has to be returned. Suppose you want to sell your business? If you don't have any record of the loan, a prospective buyer may be scared off by an erroneous belief that there isn't any money in the business.

- **Home-equity loans** — If you own your home, it may be your biggest source of capital to start your new business. Call around for the lowest rates. Also, find out whether there are any other hidden costs you'll have to pay at closing. If you use your home for financing, consider a business loan that uses your house as collateral instead of a home-equity loan. This may enable you to write off the interest as a business expense instead of as a personal itemized deduction on your income tax.

- **Credit card loans** — Raising money by using your credit cards should be your last resort because interest rates are so high. On the other hand, credit card debt is unsecured, unlike a home mortgage that could cause you to lose your house if you default. If you find yourself in a position where this is your only choice, you should probably reevaluate your new business idea. Take a hard look at the reasons why no one is willing to lend you money. But if you really believe in yourself and in your idea, go for it. You won't be the first person to finance a successful business by using credit card debt.

Warning

A cautionary note on using credit card loans. The annual interest rate is over 18 percent on most revolving credit cards. There may be other less expensive ways to borrow money, with lower interest rates, higher credit limits and longer repayment terms. Examples include a second home mortgage or collateralized loans from banks or private credit companies.

Maximize Investment Appeal

Every small business owner is convinced the enterprise will be successful and investors can be persuaded by these convictions. However, to obtain financing, you will need to provide objective evidence your business will succeed.

Save Time

Most financiers will request certain financial statements and a business plan from you before they are willing to invest in your business. In order to be prepared for this scrutiny of your business, you should make your assessment of the creditworthiness and investor appeal of your business before you develop a business plan. While the plan should reflect your personal business goals, keep in mind who your audience is, and draft the plan so that it sells your ideas to people who are in the business of making money.

On the most basic level, every potential lender or investor evaluates a new business by looking at how the cash will be used and how the money either will be repaid or result in a profitable return. Many of these questions may be answered by data contained in your business's financial statements and projections; however, lenders and investors also make more subjective evaluations of you and your company. These assessments may affect your financing requests even more than the objective numbers.

For example, when you make the case that your business is a worthy investment, keep in mind most lenders and investors are followers, not leaders, and the best evidence of a good investment will be your prior success in raising capital.

Work Smart

Additional evidence of future success for your business can sometimes take the form of contract commitments from existing or prospective customers, industry or professional opinions, and market research—even if it's informal testimonials. In your business plan or loan application, make sure to note any advantageous market trends, consumer appeal, management experience, retention of skilled employees and availability of any special resources (e.g., a valuable patent). Identifying a lender whose strategic approach or special industry focus matches your business will also enhance the subjective appeal of your business.

A financier wants to spread risk as much as possible, and a certain comfort level may be reached if other investors have a significant vested economic interest in your business. If you can show a strong financial commitment to the business from additional investors, as well as a meaningful personal investment by the business owners, the appeal of your company will correspondingly increase.

Your past business experiences, expertise and managerial skills likewise play a crucial factor in determining the appeal of your business. If you can establish a personal relationship with a particular financier, such as a local community banker, your past successes and business experience are more apt to be considered in determining the likely future success of your business. Use your personal resume, as well as letters of reference from community professionals and businesspersons, to help project yourself as a reputable, reliable and creative businessperson.

Work Smart

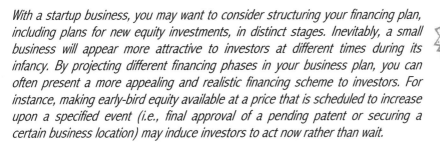

With a startup business, you may want to consider structuring your financing plan, including plans for new equity investments, in distinct stages. Inevitably, a small business will appear more attractive to investors at different times during its infancy. By projecting different financing phases in your business plan, you can often present a more appealing and realistic financing scheme to investors. For instance, making early-bird equity available at a price that is scheduled to increase upon a specified event (i.e., final approval of a pending patent or securing a certain business location) may induce investors to act now rather than wait.

Getting Additional Startup Money

Finding the money needed to start a new business is almost always one of the most difficult obstacles new owners face. At this point, your most likely sources of investment already have been mentioned, but there are some institutional possibilities as well.

Without a previous track record in business, securing a loan may be difficult. Still, it can be done. To increase your chances, consider running the business part-time until the enterprise proves itself. In some cases, local governments or community agencies may make small loans available to businesses based on only the owner's business plan and good credit, but this is pretty rare.

Here's an overview of the additional financing available to you. For a more detailed discussion, we strongly suggest you review the material on business financing either in our book *Small Business Financing: How and Where To Get It* or on our *Business Owner's Toolkit* web site at www.toolkit.cch.com.

Equity vs. Debt

A brief overview of the basic types of financing may be helpful to understanding which options might be most attractive and realistically available to your particular business. Typically, financing is categorized into two fundamental types:

- **Debt financing** — This means borrowing money that is to be repaid over a period of time, usually with interest. Debt financing can be either short-term (full repayment due in less than one year) or long-term (repayment due over more than one year). The lender does not gain an ownership interest in your business, and your obligations are limited to repaying the loan. In smaller businesses, personal guarantees are likely to be required on most debt instruments; commercial debt financing thereby becomes synonymous with personal debt financing.

- **Equity financing** — This describes an exchange of money for a share of business ownership. This form of financing allows you to obtain funds without incurring debt: in other words, without having to repay a specific amount of money at any particular time. The major disadvantage to equity financing is the dilution of your ownership interests and the possible loss of control that may accompany a sharing of ownership with additional investors.

Debt and equity financing provide different opportunities for raising funds, and a commercially acceptable ratio between debt and equity financing should be maintained. From the lender's perspective, the debt-to-equity ratio measures the amount of assets or "cushion" available for repayment of a debt in the case of default.

Excessive debt financing may impair your credit rating and your ability to raise more money in the future. If you have too much debt, your business may be considered overextended, risky and unsafe as an investment. In addition, you may be unable to weather unanticipated business downturns, credit shortages or an interest rate increase if your loan's interest rate floats.

Conversely, once your business has been operating for a while, too much equity financing can indicate you are not making the most productive use of your capital—as leverage for obtaining cash. On the other hand, building very little personal ownership equity in a business may suggest the owner isn't committed to the operation.

Lenders will consider the debt-to-equity ratio in assessing whether the company is being operated in a sensible, creditworthy manner. Generally speaking, a local community bank will consider an acceptable debt-to-equity ratio to be between 1:2 and 1:1. For startup businesses in particular, the owners need to guard against cash flow shortages that can force the business to take on excess debt, thereby impairing the business's ability to subsequently obtain needed capital for growth.

Warning

Exercise caution when making equity contributions of personal assets (cash or property) to your business. Usually, your rights to that contribution become secondary to the rights of business creditors if the business goes bad. Alternatives to outright transfers of capital to the business may be secured loans or "straw man" transactions (you loan money to a third-party relative or friend who then loans the funds to the corporation). The insider then takes a secured interest in the property.

Sources of Loan Money

Securing the proper loan—one that is affordable for, and later profitable to, your business—can sometimes be rather difficult. Depending on the profile and particular requirements of your new business, discussed throughout this chapter, some options will be a better fit than others.

Bank loans — Commercial lenders tend to shy away from new small businesses because they believe the risks of failure are too high. They want to see a history of success and a solid credit record. Thus, a lot of small businesses needing to borrow funds to get started find themselves in a classic Catch-22: The bank won't lend them money unless they have a solid track record, but they can't build the record until they get the money. What to do?

One possible solution is to look to smaller lenders with good reputations for small business lending. Bank mergers and consolidations have forced some of the smaller banks to take some chances they perhaps wouldn't have taken before. Small businesses are often the beneficiaries of those changes.

The cost of taking out a small business loan will vary from lending institution to lending institution. Call around for the best rates. Ask your friends and acquaintances for their recommendations. Each year, the Small Business Administration (SBA) publishes a report rating commercial banks on their small business lending performance (http://www.sba.gov/financing).

Federal government loans/guarantees — For many small businesses, government assistance can make the difference in getting the money they vitally need to start their operations. The SBA is a federal agency that offers a number of financing and operations assistance programs to small businesses. Through the SBA, banks will approve small business loans they would otherwise turn down, and the cost of the loan may be lower.

Currently, there are three basic financing programs that remain available through the SBA: the Microloan program for small business loans under $35,000, the Section 7(a) loan guarantee program, and the Section 504 Community Development Corporation tax credit program. Over the years, these programs have helped to provide billions of dollars in long-term credit and other financial assistance through the SBA's network of participating banks, non-bank lenders, certified development companies and SBA-licensed companies.

- The Microloan program is perhaps the most accessible to startup businesses. Microloan funds are SBA grants to approved, nonprofit organizations that accept loan applications and make loan decisions.

- The Section 7(a) loan guarantee program includes a variety of separate specialized programs, but the most popular has been "LowDoc." This program was implemented in 1993 to increase the availability of small loans (under $150,000) to businesses by reducing the paperwork previously required for an SBA loan guarantee. The SBA LowDoc application is a one-page form that, on one side, has the applicant's SBA loan application and, on the other side, has the lender's request for an SBA guarantee.

- The Section 504 program involves SBA participation in private, nonprofit companies (Certified Development Companies or "CDCs") established for the purpose of providing long-term, fixed-asset financing to small businesses.

Save Time

The SBA has offices located throughout the country. For the one nearest you, consult the telephone directory under "U.S. Government," call the Small Business Administration's Answer Desk at 1-800-8ASK-SBA (1-800-827-5722) or visit their web site at www.sba.gov/regions/states.

State and local government loans/guarantees — This form of assistance varies from location to location. Many of these agencies will have some type of an economic development program, from providing economic information to giving low-interest loans and forgivable grants.

To find out what is available in your state, contact your state department of economic development for eligibility requirements. The city and county governments are also a source of assistance. To find out what is available in your area, look in the local government section in the telephone book.

Another potential form of assistance may come from local nonprofit economic development agencies. If your community has an economic development agency, this may be your best source of obtaining information on a complete package for the new business. These agencies may assist you with some of your research, along with providing financial assistance. The local economic development offices at the city and county levels will also help identify those specific area banks most experienced with SBA loans or willing to work with small businesses and startups.

Work Smart

The loan department at your bank also may be a valuable resource in identifying state, local and agency assistance for the new businessperson. They may have gone through the steps with other new businesses in your area.

Another suggestion is to call the regional or national Department of Housing & Urban Development (HUD) office. They may provide job and other grants to startups and small businesses for job creation in the form of low-interest loans, often in conjunction with the SBA. HUD will be able to provide the names and phone numbers of local city, county and state organizations in your area that represent HUD for development of targeted geographic urban areas. For a list of contact information, visit their web site at www.hud.gov.

Franchisor loans — If your new business is going to be a franchise operation, then look to the franchisor as a financing source. A reputable franchisor will generally assist you, the franchisee, in obtaining financing for a franchise. In many instances, the franchisor will be the source of the financing or will be able to refer you to the specific lenders they use. Lenders are more inclined to provide financing to well-known franchises because they are less risky than businesses started from scratch. (For more on franchising, see Chapter 5.)

Sources of Creative Financing

Finally, there are some avenues of creative financing available to the new small business owner. Depending on your business's unique profile, these options may prove to be more beneficial than using the more traditional means of raising money.

Private investors/business angels — A less-formal source for external equity financing is through private investors, called angels, who are seeking new business investments for a variety of economic and personal reasons. Although angels tend to be less demanding in their financing terms, you should still exercise great caution in ensuring that your angel financier doesn't turn out to be a devil in disguise.

No standard angel profile exists, but these investors are often individuals or groups of either local professionals or businesspersons who are interested in assisting new businesses that will enhance the immediate community. They are not typically interested in controlling the business, although they usually want an advisory role. In addition, they may make financing contingent upon the business's adherence to certain goals or practices.

Most entrepreneurs already recognize that potential angel investors for their business might be just about anywhere. Networking within your community and your business circles can often provide a good starting point. Potential financing contacts can arise through your business associates, affiliations with relevant trade associations, inquiries through your local banker, accountant or attorney, local Chambers of Commerce and fellow small business entrepreneurs.

Work Smart

When looking for angel investors, do your best to shop for "smart money"; in other words, try to get more from an angel than just financing. Many angels will serve as advisors, or on a board of advisors, to offer the value of their experience and strategic advice on operating the enterprise. In addition, the angels will frequently use their own connections to assist the business in finding additional financing growth opportunities, favorable suppliers, new customers, etc.

The terms of angel financing depend entirely on what you can negotiate with a particular investor, but almost any type of debt or equity financing is a possibility.

In addition to your own efforts at finding interested investors in your community, you can take advantage of a growing cottage industry of angel network firms that will match up prospective investors with small businesses. Angel network firms solicit background information from entrepreneurs and investors who subscribe to their service. The network firms make their money by charging a subscription fee to each entrepreneur and investor for inclusion in their matchmaking database.

Work Smart

A number of these firms exist, including the Technology Capital Network at the Massachusetts Institute of Technology (telephone 617-253-2337; www.tcnmit.org) and the Capital Network Events in Austin, TX (telephone 512-305-0826; www.cnevents.com). The Small Business Administration also offers a service called ACE-Net, which is an angel network on the Internet at https://ace-net.sr.unh.edu/pub/.

Leasing — Leasing companies, as well as banks and some suppliers and vendors, will rent equipment and other business assets to small businesses. Some manufacturers have leasing agents who may be able to arrange lease terms or a credit arrangement with the manufacturer, a subsidiary company or a specific lessor.

Leasing assets, rather than purchasing them, is a form of financing because it avoids the large down payment frequently required for asset purchases and frees up funds for other business expenditures. However, you should be aware leasing from conventional lenders may be difficult for startup businesses because traditional lenders require an operating history from prospective lessees.

Among the advantages of leasing: Cash is freed up for other purposes, less debt appears on your financial statements, equipment changes or upgrades can be more easily acquired (depending on the terms of the agreement), costs are tax-deductible, and the lessor may be willing to privately finance improvements to the property you are looking to lease (saving money on your up-front expenditures).

Because more businesses are using leases, greater creativity in lease terms and purposes are becoming available. Some leases now resemble long-term purchases of capital equipment. The lease term approximates the expected useful life of the asset, and the total lease payments are keyed to the underlying cost of the asset. The lessee pays insurance and taxes on the asset, and this type of "financing lease" is treated as a purchase for tax and accounting purposes. This treatment negates some of the advantages of leasing. Also, the lessee either may be required or have the option to purchase the asset at the end of the lease. A service contract can usually be purchased for an additional charge.

Work Smart

As your ownership options/rights are increased in a lease agreement, your financial statements may have to show the lease as an asset purchase, with an accompanying listing of the asset and a liability for the amount of the "loan." These changes will negatively affect your debt/equity ratios and your net income.

Trade credit — Your suppliers and your customers represent possible sources of financing through a variety of credit and pricing options. Trade credit is the generic term for a buyer's purchase of supplies or goods from a seller (supplier) who finances the purchase by delaying the payment due date or allowing installment payments.

Vendors and suppliers are often willing to sell on credit, and this source of working capital financing is very common for startup businesses. Suppliers know that most small business rely primarily upon a limited number of suppliers and that small businesses typically represent relatively small order risks; as long as the supplier keeps a tight rein on credit terms and receivables, most small businesses are a worthwhile gamble for future business.

Startup businesses may benefit from shopping for prospective suppliers. Many new businesses rely heavily upon a single supplier with whom they can reach a long-term understanding regarding credit purchases. Present your proposal to several possible suppliers, taking care to outline how much inventory you need to get started and how much you will buy from the supplier in the future. Expect the supplier to demand a priority security interest in all goods provided to you on credit. You also may have to personally guarantee some of the purchase price, at least for initial inventory. The more business you do with a particular seller, the better your negotiating position for arranging additional credit purchases.

Work Smart

When managing the amount of trade credit and other debt your business assumes, the critical feature is not the total amount of debt, but rather the ability of your business to make payments from its cash flow. The duration of the pay period and the repayment amounts, in relation to incoming cash sources, are most important. Realistic cash flow projections and a strong cash flow history are consequently the primary interest of trade creditors.

The major advantages of trade credit: It is often readily available, it allows you to spread your payments over several months or years, and a minimal (or no) down payment or interest charges are assessed.

The cost of trade credit is usually a higher purchase price. Keep in mind that vendors often experience the same cash flow pressures as small businesses, and many sellers offer cash discounts for immediate payment. By purchasing on credit, you forego the cash discount price and pay a higher relative price for your goods.

Opening early — This may seem very obvious, but the sooner you can open your doors to paying customers, the better off your financial situation will be. However, some may have the misconception that a business must be completely set up before it officially opens. That simply is not true. Also, opening early may be your only available option if other financing options aren't available.

As long as you can pull customers in and complete your transactions with them, you can start making the money you so desperately need. For a service industry, that may involve a means of communication and the ability to provide the service. For a retail store, that may mean a functioning store location, minimal stock on hand, and the ability to ring up a sale. At the same time, don't forget to factor in your customers' varying tolerances for a "pardon our dust" type of atmosphere.

Opening early also helps your bottom line from a tax perspective. The IRS requires you to amortize and deduct your startup expenses over a period of at least 60 months. Expenses incurred after the business begins operation, however, are often deductible in the first year. Thus, it's often a good idea to postpone some expenses until after your first customer arrives. For a more detailed examination of these tax issues, please consult our *CCH Business Owner's Toolkit Tax Guide* book or visit our web site at www.toolkit.cch.com.

TEMPERING YOUR RISK

For whatever reason, after assessing your business's affordability and opening costs, you may decide jumping into a new venture with both feet is too risky. But don't give up hope; there are ways you can reduce the risk by sticking in one toe to test the waters first. These are common ways business owners try to increase their chances for success.

Family-Operated Businesses

The majority of new small businesses involve the owner's family in some way, from letting the spouse do the bookkeeping to having the children work part-time after school. Getting family help can be a great, not to mention inexpensive, way to help you get through the startup phase. And family members make reliable fill-ins, if you get tied up with something else.

But there are other considerations: If your spouse works with you full-time, how will that affect your home life? Are you willing to, or capable of, firing a family member, if necessary? If your child or spouse is not capable of adequately doing the job, what will you do? Also, non-family employee relations need to be examined: When it is time to promote an employee, will it automatically be the family member? What is the impact?

Franchising

A good way to reduce your risk of failure is to purchase a franchise, because these businesses, at least the well-established ones, typically have a higher success rate than other types of small businesses. Successful franchisors have developed formulas for starting a new business. The good franchisors want your new business to succeed. If you fail, they fail.

Normally, when you purchase a franchise, you must follow guidelines on what you have to do as a franchisee. These will decrease your startup errors. The franchisor will provide you with facts and figures on site specifications, the maximum payout for your location and other useful information. (For more details on franchising, see Chapter 5.)

Hiring a Manager

If you're uncertain about your ability to run a small business, one good way to offset that concern is to hire someone to run it for you. This accomplishes two purposes. First, the manager can bring instant experience to the new business; second, if you have another job, you'll be able to continue with your current employment and have something to fall back on if your new business fails.

But a few words of caution: Your new business will be only as good as your new manager. If you hire a bad one, your new business may never recover from it. Also, hiring a new manager can be expensive, especially if you want one with experience in the field. Just make sure the benefits outweigh the costs.

Finally, there really isn't such a thing as a part-time small business. Even if you hire a competent manager, you'll be amazed at how much time your small business will demand of you. So be prepared to work long hours in addition to those you put in on your other job.

Using a Home Office

Operating a small business from your home is a low-risk, cost-saving alternative for some people. You can save on rent and other costs associated with opening a business outside the home. In some instances, home-office startup costs will be next to nothing, thus minimizing your financial risk in starting the new business. Also, if your new business is not a success, the shutdown costs should be minimal. For example, if you were renting outside space on a five-year lease, you potentially would be responsible for the balance of the lease payments even after your business closes its doors.

Starting Part-Time

For those who are unsure about whether they can make a go of a new business, starting out on a part-time basis is a viable alternative. It will significantly reduce your new financial risk while you gain the experience you need. And, of course, if the business fails, you can fall back on your full-time job. Also, going into a part-time new business will enable you to work out the kinks of your new business before operating on a full-time basis.

Remember, a part-time business usually will not generate a large profit. And just because you consider your new venture part-time, the related costs of doing business do not necessarily go down. In some instances, a person may be able to live off of a part-time business, but this is not usually the case. Finally, you'll be surprised at how much time a "part-time" business will take, even if you have only one client or customer. If you decide to work part-time, be prepared to work long hours.

Example

An example of a part-time business is doing paid work for friends or family on the weekends or in your spare time. Others choose to start with only a single client or customer, and use vacation time to provide the service.

Knowing When To Cut Your Losses

Part of tempering your risk in a new business requires asking yourself a difficult question: How much money am I willing to lose in this new venture? You should set a maximum dollar amount you're willing to commit. If you don't decide the financial commitment to your new business in advance, you may regret it in the future.

For example, suppose you have $50,000 in cash and investments accumulated from past saving. You're going to open a new business, and you've set your personal cash-commitment limit at $10,000. Some time later, the business is losing money and needs additional funding. What will you do? Will you increase your cash commitment or will you consider it time to cut your losses? If your business has lost the $10,000 you committed, you might be wise to stop at that amount.

Work Smart

Don't start throwing money into a sinking ship. Make sure you've made the appropriate changes to your new business to make it a successful operation. Don't just presume the business will get better.

How long are you willing to commit to an operation that will barely support itself? Would your time be better spent starting another new business related to your current idea or would you be better off becoming an employee for someone else? Before you start your new business, it would be a good idea if you also have time-commitment goals as well. For example, if you're willing to develop your business for three years and then expect a livable profit, what will you do if you have not made your profit objectives? You need to answer that question before you start your new business.

Finally, if your business does fail, do you have a fallback position? To avoid personal financial pain, you'll need to start earning some income to keep your carefully constructed personal budget on track. You may have some loans or debts that must be repaid. If you let your life savings or retirement fund go down the drain with the business, you haven't left yourself in a very good position. Nobody likes to think about or plan for failure, but you must be ready to face the unpleasant or unexpected.

Part II

Making The Crucial Choices

You've finally cleared the preliminary hurdles. You're no longer just *thinking* about launching your first small business—you're going to do it. You've assessed your skills and taken steps to fortify your weaknesses. You've researched business ideas and explored their market opportunities. And you've done a personal and professional financial analysis to determine if you can afford to strike out on your own.

Up to this point, your quest for a new business has been concerned with the intangibles—that is, you've been brainstorming ideas and possibilities. Which is not to say you haven't invested a significant amount of time and money while doing your research (and we hope you have).

But now it's time to make some very concrete decisions regarding the organizational structure of your business idea. What you decide will lay the foundation for building your new business. If you don't make the right choices now, your good idea may never become anything more than that.

How do you do that? Information is the key. The more you know about the various options in types and forms of businesses, and the numerous processes involved in properly running them, the better your odds of making it into that elite group known as successful new business owners.

In this second part of the book, we'll explore the various ways in which a business can be operated as well as who to turn to for sound guidance when making these crucial choices.

Chapter 4: Picking Professionals To Help You lets you know you're not alone—and you shouldn't be. No small business owner can do it all, so hiring the right professional help is vital to your new business. Various types of services are out there, and we'll go through the process of determining who to add to your team.

Chapter 5: Should You Start, Buy or Franchise? provides an overview of the alternatives to starting a new business from scratch. Buying an existing business or purchasing a franchise are both viable options for a brand-new entrepreneur, but each has its pros and cons. Special emphasis is placed on researching these opportunities to make sure you cut the best deal.

Chapter 6: Choosing the Form Your Business Will Take looks at the kinds of organizational forms allowed under current law as well as their tax implications. Specific documents and agreements may need to be filed. Understanding the advantages and disadvantages of each entity will allow you to make an informed choice when organizing your business.

Chapter 4

Picking Professionals To Help You

Nearly everyone who opens a business will need the assistance of an accountant, attorney, banker and insurance agent. Some also hire management or marketing consultants to take advantage of their expertise in the critical days prior to opening. If you decide you need the help of a professional (and we believe *all* prospective business owners do), then finding ones with the proper expertise should be one of the first steps you take to start your new business operation. Some of the other decisions you'll be making, such as the organizational form for your business, will be easier if you already have professional help.

It's a good idea to consider the professionals you choose as members of your business's team. They differ from vendors, suppliers and others with whom you'll deal because you're paying them to look out for your interests. If you get the feeling any of your professionals views the relationship differently (e.g., they see you as a source of income and seem disinterested in providing thoughtful input), lose that person and find someone else.

The goal of this chapter is to make you aware of the types of help available and to assist you in deciding if you need these services. When selecting professionals, two general rules determine whether you should hire them: First, do they have expertise you need but personally lack; or second, if you have the expertise, can they do it more cost-effectively (in terms of time and money) than you can?

Then, once your business's needs have been assessed, the next step is to locate the professionals you need. A good place to start your search is in your own home. If you have an accountant, lawyer, insurance agent or other professional handling your personal matters, they'll probably be happy to handle your business matters, or at least refer you to another professional who has the type of expertise you need. However, don't play guinea pig for professionals handling your personal matters by being the first person to ask them to handle business matters. Hire an experienced professional who understands the specific needs of small business owners. If you don't personally know any professionals, seek referrals from friends and relatives.

Warning

Be careful about family and friends referring other family members and friends who are just starting their professional careers. They may not have the professional experience and contacts your new business needs. You really want professionals with experience pertinent to the issues involved in organizing and operating new businesses.

Also, trade associations, local Chambers of Commerce, Better Business Bureaus, Rotary Clubs and similar organizations may provide free or limited-cost services through the professionals with which they have established relationships. By joining one of these groups, you can gain access to services supplied by professionals already familiar with business needs. At a minimum, they should be able to provide referrals of those serving the organization or participating in its activities.

TYPES OF PROFESSIONAL HELP

Which professionals will you need, and what can you expect them to do to help you organize and run your business? Every small business owner needs professional expertise in each of these areas, but whether a professional needs to be hired and retained will depend on the requirements of your particular operation. Here's a quick look at the kinds of assistance you can expect from each type of professional and where to find it:

Accountant

An accountant is vital to your new business. This professional can help you set up your books, prepare your taxes, and provide you with tax advice related to the formation and operation of your business— such as how to choose the best retirement plan and how to take advantage of the amortization deductions allowed for startup expenses. In addition, an accountant can assist you in setting up the systems you need to ensure timely payment of payroll and sales taxes. And once you've been in business for a while, an accountant can help you analyze your financial results so you can better forecast where your business is heading.

To find the right accountant for your operation, ask advice of business associates and other small business owners. If you have a banker, attorney or insurance agent, ask for a recommendation. Or contact the American Institute of Certified Public Accountants (AICPA) main office at 1211 Avenue of the America, New York, NY 10036-8775; telephone 212-596-6200; www.aicpa.org. You can also get information from local professional associations (for example, your state or local CPA organization), or from your local Chamber of Commerce or Better Business Bureau. When all else fails, look in the Yellow Pages. Again, shop around and negotiate all fees in advance.

Attorney

An attorney can be very useful in helping you understand the consequences of the form of business you choose, making your decision about the type of entity an informed one. Attorneys also help you comply with the various filing requirements that apply to small businesses. If your business involves contracts and other legal documents (and almost all do—have you ever read the terms on the back of a lease, sales contract or invoice?), a lawyer can review and interpret them, advising you of your options. In the event of a legal action brought against your business, your attorney will be the one to defend you. Likewise, if you need to bring legal action against someone else, your attorney will represent you. Also, a lawyer can provide legal advice related to the operation and management of your business, such as the work rules you establish or whether you're in compliance with minimum wage and overtime laws.

Work Smart

Just as an accountant can be instrumental in establishing books and records that make it easy to keep track of your business's finances after it's up and running, a lawyer can make sure the management decisions you make prior to opening are legal and make good sense.

For example, if you're going to have employees, you need to be sure the methodology you use to hire those employees is appropriate. An attorney can advise you as to the legality of your business's job application form and explain what records you should keep to make it possible to defend against a suit by someone you chose not to hire. Good records are the key to establishing that you acted properly, and an attorney can help you set up an employee recordkeeping system that will support your actions.

Once you've chosen a lawyer, he or she may ask you to pay a retainer fee, which is a lump sum you pay up front and then draw against every time the lawyer advises you. This practice is becoming increasingly common because attorneys are growing wary of providing advice on credit to businesses that may fail before the bills are paid. Some lawyers may ask you for a retainer of as much as $2,000 or $3,000. Ask around to find out what others are paying.

Warning

Don't be scared off by a lawyer who wants a retainer. In some ways, it's a good method for budgeting your legal costs since you know up front how much you'll be spending.

Once again, to find the right attorney, consult with business associates and other small business owners. If you have a banker, accountant or insurance agent, ask for a recommendation. Or contact the American Bar Association at 750 North Lake Shore Drive, Chicago, IL 60611; telephone 312-988-5522. Also, there are numerous state and local bar organizations that can help you find an attorney. And you can check with your local Chamber of Commerce or Better Business Bureau. As is the case with accountants, you can always try the phone book if you reach a dead end with the other sources of referrals. Initial consultations are frequently, but not always, free, but be sure that's true before you make an appointment. Most lawyers want to know what they'll be asked to do before quoting a fee.

Establishing a long-term relationship with an attorney is absolutely vital. There's no way to predict when you'll be faced with a situation requiring the help of an attorney. Unfortunately, most events that trigger the need for an attorney are not going to be ones that will afford you a lot of time to shop around. Strict time limits on legal actions frequently mean your need to respond to a situation will be immediate.

Example

What would you do if a sheriff came to your place of business and served you with a summons to court? What if OSHA or the local board of health comes and forces you to close down? What if an employee assaults another employee? In each of these situations, you need immediate access to legal counsel in order to respond appropriately and avoid making the situation worse by taking actions that seem proper at the time, but which don't pass legal muster.

Banker

Even if you're starting a business solely with your own funds, you're going to need to establish a relationship with a banker. Once your business is operational, one of your first moves should be to set up a business checking account and a line of credit. Bankers are favorably impressed by those who have credit lines, but don't use them. Moreover, if you're going to need financing, this relationship will be essential. Also, a banker is equally essential if you plan to accept credit cards from your customers. In many cases, your banker will act as your silent partner, providing you with business operation advice.

Work Smart

If you don't use a bank loan to launch your new business, the services of a trusted banker still could be useful in other ways. For example, this professional may be willing to review a business plan or other financial statements necessary to raise investment money, and your banker's experience could prevent you from making a wrong move.

The best place to start your search for a business banker is at the bank where you have your personal accounts. If that doesn't work out, ask business associates and other small business owners. Generally, small community banks are much more willing to provide good service to small businesses. Or contact the Small Business Administration at 1-800-827-5722. They keep track of which banks in your area have the best small business-lending records.

Insurance Agent

As a new business owner, your insurance needs will depend upon the type of business you run. For example, a self-employed computer consultant operating out of a home office will have insurance needs that are significantly different from a 10-employee company manufacturing fireworks. Therefore, the cost of insurance also will depend upon the type of business you operate.

Your insurance agent is a critical player in the team of professionals you assemble for your business. Even if you choose to work out of your home on a part-time basis, you're likely to need additional coverage. Most homeowner's policies provide no coverage at all for incidents resulting from business operations. An insurance professional can help you integrate your personal insurance coverage with your business insurance coverage, so you have adequate protection at the lowest possible cost. An insurance agent also can help you evaluate what types of, and how much, coverage you need.

Be sure to obtain bids for a complete insurance package from several different insurance agents and companies. When comparing insurance proposals, make sure you are not inadvertently comparing apples and oranges. The competing packages must have very similar types and amounts of coverage in order for you to make the proper analysis.

Below are brief descriptions of the various types of insurance your new business may need. Remember, no two operations are alike. Some businesses may require additional types of insurance, and some may require only a few of those mentioned.

- **Business owner's insurance** — A business owner's policy protects against economic losses resulting from damage to the owner's property and from legal liability to others for bodily injury and property damage involving the business. Usually, the policy applies primarily to your business facility, not your home. But if you plan to operate a business out of your home and can't get your business covered by way of a rider to a homeowner's policy, you'll need to purchase this insurance. A business owner's policy covers the same kind of perils as the typical homeowner's policy, but does so for business property.

- **Property insurance** — This insurance covers losses arising from physical damage to or loss of use of the property, or theft losses. Remember to insure against the loss of the contents of your business, too. It is very possible to have a larger investment in machinery and equipment, inventory, and business records than in the business's building itself.

- **Business interruption insurance** — This type of insurance will pay your bills while you are out of operation for a covered loss, such as a fire. Just because your business is shut down does not mean your bills will stop. This type of insurance will also provide your business with lost-profit protection.

- **Liability insurance** — This coverage protects you if you are sued. It will pay judgments against you up to the policy limits, as well as the legal fees you incur while defending yourself. Some small businesses, such as doctors and lawyers, will also need to carry professional liability coverage, which protects the insured against lawsuits resulting from professional error.

- **Key person insurance** — This insurance includes coverage in case of the owner's or manager's death or disability. It is meant to get a company through the tough times following the loss of a key person and includes a buyout of the deceased owner's interest at the time of death.

- **Workers' compensation insurance** — This type of coverage is required by law for those small businesses with employees. It varies by state and employee job-duty classification. The cost will vary based upon the worker classification and your claims rate.

- **Health insurance** — This type of policy pays the medical bills for covered illnesses and injuries. Buying group insurance through your business can be cheaper than buying an individual policy for yourself. Because of the high costs, most small employers don't offer health insurance as an employee benefit.

- **Life and disability insurance** — These policies provide covered individuals or their families with income in the event of death (life insurance) or a disability not related to work (disability insurance). These types of insurance can be relatively inexpensive. If your business will have employees who travel extensively, you might consider travel accident insurance policies, which provide benefits if an employee is killed or disabled while traveling for business purposes.

Work Smart

As a small business owner, you'll probably need several types of business insurance. Having a different insurer for each type of coverage can be a lot of trouble, while having all of your coverage with the same insurer can be needlessly expensive. On the other hand, some insurance companies offer substantial discounts to those who choose to maintain all of their policies with a single insurer.

Your best bet may be to look for an independent insurance agent. This way, you can have one person handle all of your insurance needs, and the agent can shop around among several companies in order to find you the right coverage at the lowest rates.

Most people have some insurance, even if it's only an automobile policy and either a homeowner's or renter's policy. Consult your current agent regarding the additional coverage you'll need to protect your business. Business insurance is a rather specialized niche, and your own agent might not be able to provide you with quotes. If that's the case, see if your agent can refer you to another agency able to provide the insurance you need. If not, try asking business associates and other small business owners. Or, if you must, start looking in the phone book.

Another source that may be more focused, more experienced and less expensive is your industry association. These associations usually provide a large, predictable, homogenous pool for underwriters, which generates lower rates. They can often provide one-stop shopping for both business and personal insurance needs (e.g., liability, property and contents, life, medical, etc.).

Management and Marketing Consultant

A good consultant (one with substantial startup experience) can be a valuable source of basic business formation and operation advice. Many of the traps for the unwary can be avoided by getting the help of someone who's been there before. For example, decisions regarding pricing, required opening inventory levels and advertising are frequently difficult ones for new business owners.

One low-cost option would be to use SCORE, the Service Corps of Retired Executives. This national organization is sponsored by the Small Business Administration (SBA). With over 13,000 member volunteers, SCORE provides free counseling and workshops to new small businesses. Check the telephone directory under "U.S. Government," or visit SCORE's web site at http://www.score.org.

Warning

Even if you have legal, accounting or marketing training, you should still consider hiring an outside professional. As a new business owner, time is likely to be your most valuable asset. If you take on all the legal, accounting and marketing activities yourself, you'll have less time to devote to the day-to-day activities leading up to opening your business. If you put a reasonable dollar value on your time, you may find that it's less expensive and less disruptive to hire an outside professional.

USING PROFESSIONALS WISELY

Remember the personal skills assessment in Chapter 1? You need to consider the results of that exercise in light of the professional services needs for your particular business. Although you don't have to identify every possible need you'll have for professional assistance, your analysis should be sufficiently comprehensive so that you identify the classes of activities with which you may require assistance. For example, it would be foolish for any business owner to decide there was absolutely no risk of being sued as a result of something related to business activities. For better or worse, we live in a society where people frequently seek recourse through the legal system, even if more reasonable methods are available.

The reason for conducting this analysis is to enable you to make an informed decision about which services you will pay to have done professionally. Being aware of the business's needs allows you to consider suggestions from the professionals and to make the best decisions for your business. A thorough assessment also can help minimize the costs of using professionals by clearly defining what services you require. By clearly organizing the needs of your business, you will make it easier for your paid professional help to render the services your new business requires.

Chapter 5

Should You Start, Buy or Franchise?

Once you've decided you're going to launch your own business, it pays to consider all of the options available for turning your plans into reality. Many people naturally think starting a new business means just that: building something out of nothing. And it's true, many small businesses are built that way. However, in many fields, you have at least two other options. You can buy an existing business or acquire a franchise.

Both options can reduce the time and effort you'll personally expend on some startup activities. The trade-off, of course, is it'll cost you money to go one of these routes. It may not be more than you'd ultimately spend if you had started from scratch, but you'll probably have to come up with more money in advance.

Thus, if you're in the process of building a small business on little capital (like our house-painting friend doing side jobs), these options may not be so attractive. But if you can afford to buy an existing business or franchise, you definitely should consider these possibilities.

Buying an existing business is a quick way to jump into the marketplace, provided you can find the right business and get it at a reasonable price. Similarly, acquiring a franchise lets you take advantage of the resources and experience of the franchisor. Acquiring an existing, operating franchise combines both advantages. So, let's examine these options as alternatives to doing it the old-fashioned way.

BUYING AN EXISTING BUSINESS

The steps involved in buying a business are similar to those taken whenever you make any major purchase. You need to locate a good business for sale, thoroughly research it, and decide whether to buy based on the purchase price and the perceived value of the business.

Caution should be exercised throughout the whole process, not only because it will help you find the business that's right for you, but it will also help you avoid the tricks of unscrupulous sellers. Your business planner or your accountant should be actively involved in your search. If you've ever bought a used car, take what you learned about the process and apply it here. As a buyer, one of your key considerations should be why the seller wants to sell.

Work Smart

Don't bring in an attorney too early in the process—not only are they expensive, they are trained to look for problems and may present an unnecessarily pessimistic view of your target business.

Advantages of an Existing Business

- **Immediate operation** — Business can begin immediately. In many cases, you may not even need to shut down the business for any appreciable period of time in order to effectuate the change in ownership.

- **Quick cash flow** — Existing inventory and receivables can produce quick cash flow.

- **Existing customers** — Customers and suppliers already have been located, and relationships with them have been established. Although it'll be up to you to maintain these relationships, you'll have a base to work from.

- **Existing reputation** — A positive reputation or goodwill toward products or services (presumably) has been created. Even if you define goodwill as nothing more than inertia (people will come to your store because that's what they've been doing), it's a powerful factor in the purchasing process.

- **Easier financing** — Since the business has a track record, financing is easier to obtain. In many cases, you may be able to arrange seller financing.

- **Eliminate competition** — Buying may eliminate a competitor you would've had to face if you opened a new business.

Disadvantages of an Existing Business

- **Cost** — Buying a business is sometimes, but not always, more costly than starting one from scratch.

- **Problems** — There may be inherent problems in the business, some of which may not be apparent until after the sale has been completed.

- **Obsolete goods** — Inventories and equipment may be obsolete.

- **Personality conflicts** — Your personality may clash with existing managers and employees.

- **Uncollectable receivables** — Receivables may be uncollectable, meaning you won't be generating the cash flow you expected.

Save Money

When purchasing a business, don't buy the receivables, or else structure the purchase so you are reimbursed for uncollectable receivables.

Finding a Business To Buy

If you're in the market to purchase a business, there are many sources available to you to find a business for sale. If you know what type of business you want to launch, trade associations for that industry may be a good place to start your search.

If you are looking for a business in a particular area, you may want to contact the local Chambers of Commerce in that area to see if they can provide any assistance.

Some other places to look:

- **Newspapers** — From large metropolitan dailies to small local weeklies, most papers have a classified ad section in which businesses are listed for sale. Some, such as *The Wall Street Journal*, even have a specific section of businesses for sale.

- **Internet** — There are many sites listing businesses for sale, and more are appearing all the time. You can do a general search of sites offering businesses for sale, or you can do a specific search for the particular type of business you're interested in.

- **Business brokers** — Another route for finding a business is to go through a business broker who matches people wanting to buy a business with people selling one. On one hand, the broker, at least a good one, will screen businesses up for sale to determine any major problems and to make certain the operation being sold exists. Also, the broker will guide you through the process of buying and help you deal with snags that may develop along the way. On the other hand, the broker's fee to sell the business will probably result in a higher purchasing price for you, even if the seller is the one who's nominally paying this commission.

Did You Know?

 You don't have to limit your search only to businesses listed for sale. If you find a business you'd like to own, tell the owner you'd like to buy it and make an offer (subject to your attorney's approval of the contract, of course). The worst that can happen is the owner will say no.

If a particular business seems like a promising choice, you'll want to contact the owner (or the broker, if the business has been listed with a broker) to find out the general facts about the business. With this information, you'll be able to tell if you want to proceed further.

Researching the Business

After finding a business for sale that seems to be a likely prospect for success, you should spend enough time to thoroughly investigate the operation. You should definitely get your lawyer and accountant involved in this process, as well. By thoroughly investigating the business (doing due diligence, in business-speak), you increase the chances of making a decision that is right for you. The time spent investigating the business, the industry and the market will make you confident your decision to buy (or not to buy) is the right one.

In many cases, the seller will require you to sign an agreement before giving you any sensitive information regarding the business and its finances. Don't be surprised if you're asked to execute the following agreements:

- **Letter of intent** — This is a non-binding offer to purchase the business, contingent on your analysis of the information made available after you sign. The purpose is to set the basic terms of the deal and commit the parties to exploring it further.

- **Confidentiality agreement** — This is a contract that prohibits you from disclosing any of the information the seller provides or from using it for any purpose other than making a decision whether or not to buy the business. The intent is to protect the seller if you decide not to purchase the business.

Remember, if a business is for sale, there must be a reason why. That reason may be an internal business problem, such as poor cash flow or bad management. Or the reason may be external, such as a poor economy or new competitors entering the market. Of course, the reason may not involve a problem, but rather the owner's decision to retire or other personal factors. A thorough investigation should reveal any existing problems and enable you to weigh those problems in your purchasing decision.

A business investigation is usually performed before the business is bought, but can continue after the sale. In such a case, some of the sales proceeds will probably be held in escrow until the investigation is completed, or your contract may stipulate that the seller will reimburse you if certain types of problems turn up.

A proper business investigation involves taking a hard, objective look at every aspect of the operation. In many instances, however, time will not permit you to investigate as thoroughly as you would like. Yet certain basic inquiries should be made. At a minimum, you should examine the following documents:

- **Organizational documents** — The documents that show how the business is organized, such as partnership agreements, articles of incorporation and business certificates, should be examined to determine how the business is structured and capitalized.

- **Contracts and leases** — Documents such as property and machinery leases, sales contracts or purchase contracts should be examined to determine the exact obligations the business is subject to.

- **Financial statements** — Examine the financial statements for the past three years (and longer if available) to determine the financial condition of the business.

- **Tax returns** — Examine the tax returns for the past three years (and longer if available) to determine the profitability of the business and whether any tax liability is outstanding.

Asking prices for businesses are usually offered as a range, open for negotiation. So, the more thorough your research, the more prepared you'll be to determine if the price is fair. Also, your investigation lays the groundwork for your negotiation strategy, should you choose to buy.

Document Checklist

Try to obtain and examine all of the documents contained in this checklist from any business you're thinking about buying. Treat a seller's inability or unwillingness to provide this information with the greatest suspicion.

❑ Asset list including real estate, equipment and intangible assets like patents, trademarks and licenses

❑ Real and personal property documents (e.g., deeds, leases, appraisals, mortgages, loans, insurance policies, etc.)

❑ Bank account list

❑ Financial statements for the last three to five years

❑ Tax returns for as many years as possible

❑ Customer list

❑ Sales records

❑ Supplier/purchaser list

❑ Contracts that the business is a party to

❑ Advertisements, sales brochures, product packaging and enclosures, and any other marketing materials

❑ Inventory receipts (also take a look at the inventory itself, to check the amount and condition)

❑ Organizational charts and resumes of key employees

❑ Payroll, benefits, and employee pension or profit-sharing plan information

❑ Certificates issued by federal, state or local agencies (e.g., certificate of existence, certificate of authority to transact business, liquor license, etc.)

❑ Certificates, registration articles and any amendments filed with any federal, state or local agency (e.g., articles of incorporation for a corporation, articles of organization for a limited liability company, etc.)

❑ Organizational documents (e.g., corporate bylaws, partnership agreements, operating agreements for limited liability companies, etc.)

❑ List of owners, if more than one (e.g. all shareholders if a corporation, all partners if a partnership, all members if a limited liability company, etc.)

Deciding Whether To Buy the Business

Once you've found out everything you can about the business, it's time to make the final purchase decision. Here are a few questions to think about before you make the final decision:

- **Have you gathered all the information you can?** Don't be surprised if this process takes several months. Above all, don't rush into the decision until you've explored every option.

- **Did you show the gathered information to your lawyer and accountant?** Ask them if they think the purchase is a good idea, and why or why not.

- **Do you fully understand the true reason why the current owner wants to sell?** If the business hasn't been doing well, you should know precisely how to fix it. Don't buy a business on the vague hope you'll somehow magically turn it around.

- **Is your decision from the head as well as the heart?** Don't buy a business just because you've fallen in love with the idea of being your own boss or because you really like the building where the business is located. You must be able to make money.

- **Do you know how to run the business you want to buy?** If you don't, take the time to learn more about it or make arrangements for the current owner to stick around after the sale to show you the ropes. If the business is sold to someone else in the meantime, you'll still be better off than you would be if you had bought a business you didn't fully understand.

BUYING A FRANCHISE

First of all, let's define what we mean by the term franchising. It refers to an arrangement in which a party, the franchisee, buys the right to sell a product or service from a seller, the franchisor. The right to sell a product or service is the franchise.

There are basically two types of franchises: (1) product and trade-name franchises and (2) business-format franchises. A product and trade-name franchise generally involves the distribution of a product through dealers. For example, auto dealerships are product and trade-name franchises that sell products produced by the franchisor.

Business-format franchises generally include everything necessary to start and operate a business in one complete package. These provide the product, trade names, operating procedures, quality-assurance standards, management-consulting support and facility design. For example, many familiar convenience stores and fast-food outlets are franchised in this manner.

People are attracted to franchises because the best ones have proven to be extremely successful over the years, and these operations combine many of the benefits of business ownership with the brand name, experience and economies of scale provided by the established corporate franchisor. In fact, good franchises generally have a higher success rate than other types of businesses.

Advantages of Franchising

- **Minimized risk** — A reputable franchise is a proven operation.

- **Name recognition** — A well-known name can bring customers into the business and provide a competitive advantage.

- **Training** — A franchisor can provide a regimented training program to teach the franchisee about the business operation and industry, even if the franchisee has no prior experience.

- **Support** — A franchisor can provide managerial support and problem-solving capabilities for its franchisees.

- **Economies of scale** — Cost savings on inventory items can be passed on to the franchisee from bulk purchase orders made by the franchisor.

- **Advertising** — Cooperative advertising programs can provide national exposure at an affordable price.

- **Financing** — A franchisor will generally assist the franchisee in obtaining financing for the franchise. In many instances, the franchisor will be the source of financing. Lenders are more inclined to provide financing to franchises because they generally are less risky than businesses started from scratch.

- **Site selection** — Most franchises will assist the franchisee in selecting a site for the new franchise location.

Disadvantages of Franchising

- **Franchise fees** — Paid to the franchisor at the inception of the franchise agreement, these fees can range from a few thousand to hundreds of thousands of dollars, depending on the franchise.

- **Royalties** — The cost of many franchises includes a monthly royalty (fee) based on a percentage of the franchisee's income or sales, and you pay even if the business is not profitable.

- **Loss of control** — Franchise agreements usually dictate how the franchise operates. The franchisee must adhere to the standards in the franchise agreement, which thereby leaves the franchisee with less control over the operation.

- **Required purchases** — The franchisor may require the franchisee to purchase certain materials for the purpose of producing uniform franchise products.

- **Termination clause** — The franchisor may retain the right to terminate the franchise agreement if certain conditions are not met. The franchisor then could end the agreement and offer the franchise location to another buyer.

Franchise vs. New Business

In deciding between purchasing a franchise and starting a new business, perhaps the best place to begin is to ask yourself why you want to own a business. The answers you give may provide some insight into which path you should choose.

- **You want to be your own boss** — If you want to launch your own business because of the freedom it will bring, you probably shouldn't buy a franchise. If you buy a franchise, the franchisor will dictate much of what you have to do, when you do it and how you do it. You'll have far more control if you start your own business.

Warning

A lot of people in the franchising field will tell you franchises have a failure rate of about 5 percent, compared to the 50 percent failure rate of independent entrepreneurs.

However, there are studies that question this 5 percent rate. For example, a 1995 study by Dr. Timothy Bates, a professor at Wayne State University in Detroit, found the franchise failure rate actually exceeded 30 percent and franchisees made lower profits than independent entrepreneurs. Dr. Bates' study also found the average capital investment of franchisees was $500,000, compared to $100,000 for independent entrepreneurs.

- **You believe you have an idea with a lot of promise** — If you want to nurture your idea into full bloom, you probably shouldn't buy a franchise. You won't have much control or be given much of an opportunity to pursue your ideas (try telling McDonald's that their golden arches ought to be bright green). You may be better off starting your own business.

- **You want to make lots of money** — If you want to launch your own business because of the financial opportunities it presents, you should look long and hard at franchising. Franchises don't necessarily make more money than other types of businesses, but they may have higher success rates. Of course, you'll be paying for the higher success rate in the fees sent to the franchisor.

- **You have money but want something to keep you busy** — If you readily possess the startup funds, a franchise may be ideal for you, particularly if you lack hands-on experience. You'll get help with everything you need to set up your business: site selection, inventories, management counseling, hiring practices and every other necessary function for the operation of your business.

Did You Know?

Franchises are particularly popular among downsized business executives and early retirees because they fit the ideal franchise profile: They often have startup money in hand, but little experience in the industry.

Franchise vs. Existing Business

Deciding whether to buy a franchise or an existing business is even more difficult than the choice between a franchise and a new startup business. The difficulty lies in the fact that both the franchise and the existing business have many similarities, such as:

- **Winning track record** — Both are (presumably) successful business concepts. If they weren't successful, you wouldn't be considering them now.

- **Greater startup costs** — Both will cause you to pay a premium for the successful business concept. A franchise may be more costly due to its previous history of success.

- **Name recognition** — The existing business will have at least local name recognition, while the franchise may have local and even national name recognition.

- **Management support** — This should be inherent in the franchise purchase. On the other hand, it generally isn't included in the purchase of an existing business, but can be structured into the deal by retaining the seller to stay on as a consultant for a period of time.

There are a few things the franchise will provide that the existing business will not:

- **Continuous management support** — One of the core concepts of a franchise is that the franchisor provides management support for the life of the franchise. Even if a seller has agreed to remain as a consultant for an existing business, that consulting arrangement is for a limited period of time. After the consulting arrangement ends, the buyer is on his or her own.

- **Greater exposure** — A franchise will usually provide greater exposure to new customers through national advertising campaigns and name recognition.

- **Shared costs** — Expenses for each franchise, such as advertising, may be pooled to take advantage of group discounts.

- **Less risk** — Franchising succeeds only if the individual franchisees are successful. Thus, the franchises are usually packaged in a manner that will enable them to succeed. The franchises are generally based in whole or in part on previously successful franchise arrangements. In comparison, an existing business may not have any history other than its current one. Even though an existing business is successful for the current owner, that success may not transfer over to another owner.

- **Complete business methodology** — A franchise can provide a training program to teach about the business operation and industry, even if the franchisee has no prior experience.

In choosing between a franchise and an existing business, you'll have to decide whether these extra features are worth the added cost.

Finding a Franchise

If you're considering buying a franchise, there are several places you can look. If you know which franchise you're interested in, the most obvious place to start is with the franchisor. They can give you all the information you'll need about purchasing a franchise.

An alternative that isn't so obvious, but can achieve the same result, and possibly at a savings, is to contact existing franchisees who are looking to sell their franchises. You may save money because you are not paying the franchisor a fee since you are taking over an existing franchise.

However, you may pay the equivalent of a franchise fee to the franchise seller if the seller is asking a premium for the franchise being sold. You can determine whether the premium is reasonable by comparing it to the fee for a new franchise. Also, a franchisor may be able to provide you with the name of an existing franchisee who is looking to sell. Finally, some franchisors may buy back and operate franchises from franchisees until they can find a suitable buyer.

Another good place to look is at annual franchising trade shows. These shows provide an opportunity to talk with many franchisors and industry experts in one location. Often, the shows will have seminars to educate potential franchisees on what they can expect as well as the advantages and disadvantages of being a franchisee. Details of trade shows can be obtained on the Internet at Trade Show Central at http://www.tscentral.com.

You can also find franchises for sale in the same places you would look when searching for any business to buy—in newspapers, over the Internet or through business brokers (see page 74).

Researching the Franchise

Buying a franchise, like making any other major purchase, should involve a thorough investigation. The time spent investigating the franchise, the industry and the market will make you confident your decision to buy (or not to buy) is the right one. In general, a prospective franchise should have an established reputation, sufficient capital, high-quality products or services, and satisfied franchisees.

What To Ask

A reference list of current and former franchisees should be available from the franchisor. (If a reference list isn't available, be cautious!) Try to determine whether the franchisor is attempting to expand the number of franchisees as quickly as possible (which may be at the expense of existing franchisees).

When researching a franchise, get answers to as many of these questions as you can before making a decision. Keep in mind this is not an exhaustive list, but a starting point identifying the main items.

- Is there a prototype location that is the basis for the franchising operation?

- Is the franchise too dependent on the founders of the franchise?

- Is there a strong management team of officers, directors and consultants who understand the industry and the use of franchising as a means of expanding the business?

- Is there enough capital to support the franchising program and provide assistance to franchisees?

- Is there a recognized and distinctive trade identity that is a registered trademark? Does the franchise have a uniform trade appearance and overall image?

- Are the methods of operation and management proven? Have they been incorporated into an operating manual?

- Is there a comprehensive training program for franchisees?

- Is there support staff who can visit and assist franchisees?

- Is there support staff who can monitor and enforce quality control standards?

- Are there legal documents that reflect the franchise's history, strategy and policies?

- Is there a strong market for the products or services the franchise offers?

- Are there site-selection criteria based on market studies and demographic reports?

Offering Documents

A franchisor will send you something called offering documents, which is a package of materials the franchisor must provide to prospective franchisees. According to federal law, the offering documents must be given to the prospective franchisee at the first meeting with the franchisor where the purchase of a franchise is seriously discussed. In any event, the offering documents must be given to the prospective franchisee no fewer than 10 days before the franchise agreement is signed or before any cash is paid.

The federal government, as well most state governments, have rules and regulations regarding the content of the offering documents. The federal government approved a new format, called the Uniform Franchise Offering Circular (UFOC), that has been adopted by virtually every state. It requires offering documents to be written in "plain English." The UFOC and other offering documents must include the following information: the history of the franchise, the history of its owners, procedures for terminating and renewing the franchise relationship, quality controls, fee structures and financial statements.

Franchise Agreement

A franchise agreement is a contract between the franchisor and the franchisee. The agreement should balance the interests of the parties. However, in reality, if the franchisor is a well-known organization like McDonald's Corporation, the franchise agreement is going to be very favorable to the franchisor, and you more or less have to take it or leave it. If the franchise is more obscure, you'll have more opportunity to negotiate favorable terms for yourself.

There really is no such thing as a standard franchise agreement because each contract will be drafted to suit the individual situation. However, there are some basic terms that pertain to the franchisor and franchisee in most franchise agreements.

It's impossible to identify every term and issue that should be considered in every situation. However, this checklist should be a valuable tool if you're interested in a franchise. While you can use the checklist to understand and review a franchise agreement, you shouldn't sign it until you've discussed all of your options with an attorney.

Franchise Agreement Checklist

The checklist should be used in conjunction with the franchise agreement—the document that will set out all the terms and conditions that will govern your ownership of the franchise—which will be drafted by the franchisor. You can use this checklist either before you see the franchise agreement, in order to get an idea of what should be in it, or after you have a copy of the agreement, in order to review its terms.

Franchise Cost

❑   *What does the initial franchise fee purchase?*

❑   *Does it include an opening inventory of products and supplies?*

❑   *What are the payment terms: amount, time of payment, lump sum or installment, financing arrangements, etc.?*

❑   *Does the franchisor offer any financing or help in finding financing?*

❑   *Are there any deferred balances? If so, who finances and at what interest?*

❑   *Is any part or all of the initial fee refundable?*

❑   *Does the contract clearly distinguish between "total cost" and "initial fee," "initial cash required" or "initial costs," etc.?*

❑ Are there periodic royalties? If so, how much are they and how are they determined?

❑ How and when are sales and royalties reported, and how are royalties paid?

❑ If royalty payments are in whole or part payment for services by the franchisor, what services will be provided?

❑ Are accounting/bookkeeping services included or available?

❑ How are advertising and promotion costs divided?

❑ Is a specified amount of working capital required of the franchisee to cover operating costs until profits can be made?

❑ Must premises be purchased or rented, and are there further conditions on either of these (from franchisor, selected site, etc.)?

❑ How and by whom will the building be financed, if purchased?

❑ Does the franchisee have to make a down payment for construction and/or equipment?

Franchise Location

❑ Does the franchise apply to a specific geographical area? If so, are boundaries clearly defined?

❑ Who has the right to select the site?

❑ Will other franchisees be permitted to compete in the same area, now or later?

❑ Is the territory an exclusive one, and is it permanent or subject to reduction or modification under certain conditions?

❑ Does the franchisee have a first-refusal option as to any additional franchises in the original territory if it is not exclusive?

❑ Does the franchisee have a contractual right to the franchisor's latest products or innovations? If so, at what cost?

❑ Will the franchisee have the right to use his or her own property and/or buildings? If not, will the franchisor sell or lease property to the franchisee?

❑ Who is responsible for obtaining zoning variances, if required?

Buildings, Equipment and Supplies

❑ Are plans and specifications of the building determined by the franchisor? If so, does this control extend to selection of contractor and supervision of construction?

❑ Are there any restrictions on remodeling or redecorating?

❑ Must equipment or supplies be purchased from the franchisor or approved supplier, or is the franchisee free to make his or her own purchases?

- ❑ *When the franchisee must buy from the franchisor, are sales considered on consignment? Or will they be financed and, if so, under what terms?*

- ❑ *Does the agreement provide for continuing supply and payment of inventory (by whom, under what terms, etc.)?*

- ❑ *Does the franchise agreement bind the franchisee to a minimum purchase quota?*

- ❑ *What controls are spelled out concerning facility appearance, equipment, fixtures and furnishings, and maintenance or replacement of the same? Is there any limitation on expenditures involved in any of these?*

- ❑ *Does the franchisor have a group insurance plan? If not, what coverage will be required, at what limits and costs? Does the franchisor require that it be named as an insured party in the franchisee liability coverage?*

Operating Practices

- ❑ *Must the franchisee participate personally in conducting the business? If so, to what extent and under what specific conditions?*

- ❑ *What degree of control does the franchisor have over franchise operations, particularly in maintaining franchise identity and product quality?*

- ❑ *What continuing management aid, training and assistance will be provided by the franchisor, and are these covered by the service or royalty fee?*

- ❑ *Will advertising be local or national, and what will be the cost-sharing arrangement, if any, in either case?*

- ❑ *If local advertising is left to the franchisee, does the franchisor exercise any control over such campaigns or share any costs?*

- ❑ *Does the franchisor provide various promotional materials—point-of-purchase, mail programs, etc.—and at what cost?*

- ❑ *What are bookkeeping, accounting and reporting requirements, and who pays for what?*

- ❑ *Are sales or service quotas established? If so, what are the penalties for not meeting them?*

- ❑ *Are operating hours and days set forth in the franchise contract?*

- ❑ *Are there any limits as to what is or can be sold?*

- ❑ *Does the franchisor arrange for mass purchasing, and is it mandatory for the franchisee to be a participating buyer?*

- ❑ *Who establishes hiring procedures initially and through the franchise term?*

Termination and Renewal

❑ *Does the franchisor have the absolute privilege of terminating the franchise agreement if certain conditions have not been met, either during the term or at the end?*

❑ *Does the franchise agreement spell out the terms under which the franchisor may repurchase the business?*

❑ *Does the franchisor have an option or duty to buy any or all of the franchisee's equipment, inventory or other assets if the franchise is terminated for good cause, by either party?*

❑ *If the preceding situation occurs, how are purchase terms determined?*

❑ *Is there provision for independent appraisal? Is any weight given to goodwill or franchisee equity in the business?*

❑ *Does the original agreement include a clause that the repurchase price paid by the franchisor should not exceed the original franchise fee? If so, this eliminates any compensation for goodwill or equity.*

❑ *Under what conditions (illness, etc.) can the franchisee terminate the franchise? In such cases, do termination obligations differ?*

❑ *Is the franchisee restricted from engaging in a similar business after termination? If so, for how many years and in what geographic region?*

❑ *If there is a lease, does it coincide with the franchise term?*

❑ *Does the contract provide sufficient time for amortization of capital payments, or will a balloon payment be required?*

❑ *Has the franchisor, as required, provided for return of trademarks, trade names and other identification symbols, and for the removal of all signs bearing the franchisor's name and trademarks?*

Other Points To Consider

❑ *Can the franchisee sell the franchised business and assign the franchise agreement to the buyer?*

❑ *Is the franchise assignable to heirs, or may it be sold by the franchisee's estate on death or disability?*

❑ *Does the lease permit assignment to any permitted assignee of the franchisee?*

❑ *How long has the franchisor been doing business in its industry, and how long has it granted franchises?*

❑ *How many participating franchises and company-owned outlets are claimed? Is it verifiable?*

❑ *If there is a trade name of a well-known person involved in the franchise, is this person active, does this person have any financial interest, does this person receive compensation for work or solely for use of his/her name, etc.?*

❑ *Are all trademarks, trade names or other marks fully identifiable and distinct, and are they clear of any possible interference or cancellation owing to any pending litigation?*

❑ *What is the duration of any patent or copyright material held by the franchisor? If time is limited, does the franchisor intend to renew, and is this spelled out in the franchise agreement?*

❑ *Has the franchisor provided the franchisee with an offering document package meeting FTC rule requirements or the UFOC format?*

❑ *Are there state laws governing franchisor/franchisee relationships, including contract provisions, financing arrangements and terminations? If so, does the contract meet all requirements? Has the franchisor met all state law requirements (registration, escrow or bonding requirements, etc.), if applicable?*

Deciding Whether To Buy the Franchise

Once you have found a franchise and completed your investigation, all that's left is the final purchase decision. Here are a few questions to think about before you make that final decision:

• **Have you gathered all the information you can?** Above all, don't rush into the decision until you've explored every avenue of the franchise.

• **Did you show your gathered information to your lawyer and accountant?** Ask them if the purchase is a good idea, and why or why not.

• **Is your franchisor reputable?** When we hear "franchising," we often think "safe." But there are plenty of unscrupulous franchisors out there. Franchising is so popular these days not just because people are eager to buy, but also because people are so eager to sell them. There is a lot of money to be made by those who sell franchises. Consequently, a lot of people, some of whom are unscrupulous, are drawn to franchising.

• **Is your decision from the head as well as the heart?** Don't buy a franchise, for example, just because you enjoy the food you eat there. Don't buy it unless you are reasonably sure you can make some money from it.

Chapter **6**

Choosing the Form Your Business Will Take

After deciding you're going to start your own business, zeroing in on the kind of company, choosing whether to start from scratch or buy an existing business or franchise, and selecting your team of advisors, your next step should be to address the issue of your new business's organizational structure. Will the new business be operated as a corporation, a sole proprietorship, a partnership or some other type of entity? In this chapter, we'll examine the reasons why different types of business organizations may be preferable in different situations, and what the trade-offs are for each type of entity.

Every business has to choose some form of organization. That may seem odd, but the state and federal governments insist on it. If you don't choose one, you will be treated as if you chose the form that most nearly matches your actual operations.

Example

Let's say John simply prints up business cards with his name and phone number, and starts his own painting business. He doesn't do anything else to formalize the existence of his business.

By default, John's business is a sole proprietorship. Whether this is the best choice depends on a variety of circumstances. If John had gone into business with a friend, sharing the income and expenses, the default form of organization would be a partnership.

Whether you've purchased an existing business or started one from scratch, you must decide which form of organization (sometimes referred to as business entity) is best for your company. The decision can be difficult to make. Be sure to consult your attorney or accountant before making a final decision. There are several choices, and each has its advantages and disadvantages. Your organizational options: sole proprietorship, partnership, corporation, S corporation, limited liability company and, in some cases, limited liability partnership.

Remember, the form you choose isn't necessarily permanent. If the circumstances of your business change, you can always change the form of your business. For example, you may start your business as a sole proprietorship, but as your business grows, you may decide you want to limit the exposure of your personal assets by converting to a corporation or an LLC. There are some restrictions (e.g., you may not be able to re-elect S corporation status for some time after you terminate an election to be an S corporation), but you definitely have a reasonable amount of flexibility.

Work Smart

Even if you think your new business should be operated as a corporation, don't incorporate too early. When you incorporate a business, you become responsible for a number of regulatory activities, such as filing annual reports with the state, paying fees imposed by the state, complying with sales and income tax reporting rules, etc. Don't take on these responsibilities until you'll derive some benefit from the corporate form.

SOLE PROPRIETORSHIPS

The easiest and least expensive way to organize a business entity is as a sole proprietorship. You simply decide to begin operating the business as a sole proprietor and it's done.

There are no documents or forms needed, unless the business will operate under a name other than the owner's name. If this is the case, most localities will require you to file a fictitious owner affidavit. This informs the local government and the public that the business is operating under an assumed name, and indicates who the owner is. (Also, you may have to file forms if you need a business license, but that's a separate issue.)

Warning

In some jurisdictions, a business legally cannot begin to operate unless the proper business license has been obtained by the owner. The same is true regarding permits. Make sure you look into both state and local requirements that may impact your business before opening your doors.

Many localities require you to publish, in local newspapers, notice that you're going to do business under a name you've chosen. The notice identifies you and indicates the name under which you'll be doing business. To find out more about the requirements in your locality, go to or call the courthouse located in your county seat. Ask for the county clerk. The clerk should be able to answer any questions you have and to give you whatever forms you may need.

Once you file your fictitious owner affidavit with the county clerk, you should, of course, keep a copy of it. You'll need it from time to time, such as when you open up a business bank account under the fictitious name.

If you operate your business under a fictitious name, make sure you file an affidavit in each county where you do business. If you do business across state lines, the rules get a little trickier because they can vary. In that event, you should definitely discuss your options with your attorney.

Work Smart

Choosing between your own name and a fictitious name can be a difficult decision. There are a couple of rules of thumb. If you're reasonably well-known and well-respected in your community or in your business field, use your own name. It can be a great marketing tool.

However, there's a risk with using your own name. If your business fails or gets into financial or legal trouble, it'll have your name on it. If you try to start another business, people may associate your name with the earlier troubles.

As owner of a sole proprietorship, you'll be personally liable for all obligations of the business. Personal liability means creditors of your business can go after your personal assets if the business assets aren't sufficient to cover the business debts. Likewise, your personal creditors can go after your business assets to satisfy your personal debts.

Therefore, you should consider whether the business will be exposed to any potential lawsuits. And most are. For example, the business can be exposed to liability for customers injured on the premises or from products sold by the business. If the possibility of lawsuits exists, you can limit your exposure by purchasing business insurance (general liability, malpractice or product liability, if necessary). As an alternative, you might want to consider a different business form that would provide greater liability protection, such as a corporation or a limited liability company.

Sole Proprietorship Tax Issues

The tax treatment of a sole proprietorship is relatively simple. Business income or loss is reported on Schedule C of the owner's individual income tax return. The owner will probably have to make estimated payments of income and self-employment taxes periodically during the year.

If the business will hire employees, a Federal Employer Identification Number must be obtained and payroll taxes will have to be paid. A Federal Employer Identification Number can be obtained by filing a Form SS-4, Application for Employer Identification Number. You may obtain a Form SS-4 by calling the Internal Revenue Service at 1-800-TAX-FORM.

Advantages of a Sole Proprietorship

- **Control** — The owner has complete control over the business operations.

- **Simplicity** — A sole proprietorship is easy to start and operate.

- **Inexpensive** — Startup organizational expenses are minimal since no legal documents need to be created to begin the enterprise.

- **No double taxation** — The business is not treated as a separate taxable entity. The business income is reported on the owner's individual tax return and is therefore only taxed once.

Disadvantages of a Sole Proprietorship

- **Liability** — The owner is personally liable for any obligations of the business.

- **Limited ownership** — A sole proprietorship by definition is limited to one person. Thus, if the owner wants to admit another owner, such as a family member or friend, the sole proprietorship would have to end. A new business arrangement, such as a partnership, would be created either by default or by intent.

Work Smart

If you aren't concerned with limiting liability because your type of business is virtually risk-free, a sole proprietorship may be the perfect vehicle in which to operate your business.

PARTNERSHIPS

There are basically four types of partnerships:

- **General partnerships** — This consists of general partners who share the management of the entity and are personally responsible for the partnership's obligations.

- **Limited partnerships** — This consists of two classes of partners: general partners and limited partners. The general partners manage the limited partnership and are personally responsible for its obligations. The limited partners are similar to shareholders of a corporation. They cannot participate in the management of the entity, but can determine only who will manage the partnership. The limited partners share in the profits of the partnership, but their losses are limited to the amount of their capital contribution. Every limited partnership must have at least one general partner, who retains full personal responsibility for the partnership's obligations.

- **Limited liability partnerships** — A relatively new form of partnership structure, a limited liability partnership (LLP) is a general partnership that registers in a particular state as an LLP.

- **Limited liability limited partnerships** — This form is even more recent than an LLP. A limited liability limited partnership (LLLP) is an LLP that registers in the LLLP form.

Starting a General Partnership

If a business is going to be owned by more than one person, the simplest business form to create and operate is a general partnership. If you are considering the use of this entity form, you might want to consider electing limited liability partnership status (see page 98). Although a partnership is more complicated to form than a sole proprietorship, it is not as complicated as a corporation or limited liability company.

Forming a partnership entails an agreement between two or more prospective partners. The agreement can be oral, but should be written and signed by all partners to avoid later conflicts. Virtually anyone or any type of organization can be a partner. A partner can be an individual, a partnership, a limited liability company, a corporation or a trust.

The flexibility of a partnership allows the business to operate in a manner that best suits the business needs at the time the business starts and later when the business has matured. For example, when the business is just beginning, one partner may have skills valuable to the business, but little capital. Another partner may have capital, but not the requisite skills. The partner with skills can contribute services to the partnership while the other partner contributes capital. Later, when the business has grown, new partners can be admitted, yet their management capacity can be limited to prevent the new partners from usurping the original partners. When a partner contributes capital to a partnership, the partner receives an ownership percentage in all assets of the partnership, not just in the property contributed.

All partners are jointly and severally liable for the obligations of the partnership. Joint and several liability means each individual partner can be held responsible for all obligations of the partnership. A partner who pays an entire obligation can collect the other partners' pro rata share of the debt. Of course, the other partners may not be in a position to repay the partner.

Did You Know?

Any partner can enter into a contract on behalf of the partnership. By doing so, a partner can bind all partners in an unfavorable contract, since all partners are jointly and severally liable for the obligations of the partnership.

A partnership of two or more individuals may require the efforts of all the partners to succeed, especially in the early life of the business. If one of the partners withdraws or dies, the existence of the partnership may be threatened. To protect the partnership and the remaining partners, consider buy/sell agreements and key person life insurance policies.

A buy/sell agreement specifies how the value of a partner's interest will be determined and how it will be bought out if a partner wants to leave the partnership. Having a buy/sell agreement in place minimizes disputes over value and facilitates the purchase of the withdrawing partner's interest by the partnership, partners or new investor.

Key person life insurance is a policy on the life of key members of an organization to provide cash in the event of the death of that person. The beneficiaries are the organization or the organization members. In a partnership, key person life insurance can be purchased for all partners, or for those most active in the business or those owning the largest interests. The life insurance proceeds can be used by the partnership to keep the business going in the absence of the key partner or to buy out the deceased partner's interest pursuant to a buy/sell agreement.

As for documentation, a partnership may have to file a business certificate with the jurisdiction in which it is going to do business. If the business will operate under a name different from the owners' names, most jurisdictions will require a fictitious owner affidavit be filed. This informs the jurisdiction that the business is operating under an assumed name and indicates who the owners are. To find out what the requirements are in your jurisdiction, call your county clerk's office.

General Partnership Agreements

The partnership agreement is a complicated document that should be drafted by an attorney. State law governs these agreements, and requirements differ from state to state. At a minimum, address the following subjects in the partnership agreement:

- **Contributions** — Specify the amount and timing of contributions to be made by each partner.

- **Management and control** — Identify whether some or all partners will manage and control the partnership.

- **Profit and loss** — Specify how the profits and losses will be allocated to the partners.

- **Distributions** — Indicate when distributions of cash or property will be made.

- **Partner's responsibilities and duties** — Describe the activities and responsibilities of each partner.

- **Withdrawal** — Identify how a partner's interest will be valued if the partner withdraws from the partnership.

- **Death of a partner** — Identify how a partner's interest will be valued if the partner dies.

Additional topics to be included in the agreement, if applicable:

- **Admission of new partners** — Indicate the process for admitting new partners into the partnership.

- **Right of first refusal** — Specify if the partnership or individual partners will have the right to purchase a withdrawing partner's interest before the partner can offer to sell the interest to someone outside the partnership. Be sure to include a method for valuing the interest.

- **Duration of the partnership** — Indicate the life of the partnership along with any events that may cause the partnership to dissolve prematurely.

- **Continuation of the partnership** — Identify the criteria enabling the partners to continue the partnership if an event occurs that would otherwise cause dissolution of the partnership.

Partnership Tax Issues

A partnership is an unincorporated business with two or more owners. For businesses with more than one owner, the IRS will presume that your business should be taxed as a partnership unless you have incorporated under state law, or you elect to be taxed as a corporation by filing IRS Form 8832, *Entity Classification Election.*

Unlike a corporation, the partnership itself is not taxed. All partnership income or loss is passed to the partners and is reported on their individual income tax returns at their own individual tax rates, according to an agreed-upon allocation of interests. For example, capital gains would flow through the partnership to each partner, and then would be reported as such on the individual's return.

All income must be reported as distributed, whether or not the partners actually received their shares, or even if the money is retained in the business as partnership capital. For losses, a partner may not deduct an amount in excess of his or her total personal investment.

Partnerships are generally the most flexible form of organization for tax purposes. The taxable income, losses or other tax items distributed to the partners do not need to be divided equally, as long as a business purpose other than tax avoidance can be shown for the split. For example, one partner can receive 40 percent of any profits but 60 percent of any losses. Because new businesses frequently experience temporary losses, the pass-through tax treatment of a partnership can often benefit a partner by allowing him or her to immediately apply any losses from the business to offset income from other sources.

Even though taxes are paid individually, the partnership is required to file a tax return (Form 1065) reporting income and loss to the IRS, as well as how the distribution was divided among the partners (Schedule K-1).

Finally, for all partnerships, even if the operation has no employees, a Federal Employer Identification Number must be obtained by filing a Form SS-4. You may obtain a Form SS-4 by calling the Internal Revenue Service at 1-800-TAX-FORM.

Advantages of a General Partnership

- **Multiple owners** — More than one person can own and operate the business, unlike a sole proprietorship.

- **Simplicity** — A partnership is easy to form and operate.

- **Flexibility** — This organizational form is flexible enough to adapt to the business's changing needs.

Disadvantages of a General Partnership

- **Unlimited liability** — Each partner is jointly and severally liable for all obligations of the partnership.

- **Ease of dissolution** — The partnership agreement dissolves upon the death or withdrawal of a partner, unless safeguards are in place.

Warning

For small business owners who still *want to operate in the form of a general partnership, here is some general advice:* Don't do it. *The general partner experiences all of the same exposures to liability as the sole proprietor,* plus unlimited, personal liability for the acts of all of his co-owners. *This should make even the biggest risk-taker reconsider that decision.*

It has been said that when the biggest accounting firms were operating as general partnerships, they relied on one asset protection strategy in particular: a whole lot of insurance. Today, all of these firms are re-organized as corporations or other similarly insulated entity structures.

Starting a Limited Partnership

As previously mentioned, in a limited partnership, the general partners operate the business and are personally liable for all its obligations, while the limited partners do not have any control over the operation, other than naming the general partners. Limited partners share in the profits of the partnership, but their losses are limited to the amount of their contributions to the partnership.

Work Smart

To achieve limited liability for the owner who is assuming the general partnership interest, it was once common strategy to make the general partner be a corporation or limited liability company (LLC) owned by the individual who otherwise would have directly owned the general partnership interest. Today, this once common strategy, which requires the creation of two entities, is obsolete. The same objective, limited liability for all of the owners, can be accomplished through the use of one entity—the LLC.

A limited partnership is a creature of state statute. As such, a limited partnership does not exist until the requirements specified in the state law are met. Generally, a certificate of limited partnership is required to be signed and filed with the secretary of state's office (in some instances a limited partnership agreement also is required to be filed). The certificate contains information about the limited partnership such as its name, address, purpose, identities of the general partners, their business address, etc. The requirements of each state vary, and if they are not met, the business will be treated as a general partnership.

Limited Partnership Agreements

A limited partnership agreement contains the same basic information as a general partnership agreement (see page 94), but addresses some additional provisions pertaining to the limited partners.

Warning

A limited partnership is generally not regarded as the best choice of entity for a new business because of the required filings and administrative complexities. For a new business with two or more working partners, a general partnership would be much easier to form.

If a limited partnership is needed at a later date, the general partnership can easily convert to a limited partnership. You may even consider another entity choice, such as the LLC.

There are some situations in which the limited partnership form for a new business may be desirable. One such instance is a business in which the owner needs to raise capital from a large number of investors yet still control the way the business is operated. If that applies to you, you might consider forming a limited partnership and selling limited partnership interests to investors, although a limited liability company can also serve this purpose while avoiding the need for any general partners.

Starting a Limited Liability Partnership

When choosing a business form, you may want to consider the limited liability partnership (LLP), one of the newest entity options. An LLP is a general partnership that registers in the LLP form according to specific state rules.

The conversion process from a general partnership to an LLP is unique in the law. The general partnership simply registers as an LLP. Technically, the old entity does not dissolve, and a new entity is not created. The old entity continues to exist, but is now subject to a new set of laws (i.e., those governing the LLP). The conversion does not trigger a taxable event because there is no change in the entity. Moreover, because of this registration process, none of the assets need to be re-titled, making the conversion especially simple and inexpensive.

An LLP is similar to the limited liability company (LLC). However, there are some important differences that may make the LLP an inappropriate choice for the small business owner.

In many states, owners of an LLP have only a *reduced* form of limited liability from the claims of the business's creditors. This "limited shield," as it is sometimes called, does not afford the owners the same protection they would enjoy in either the LLC or the corporation. In addition, in *many* states, the business interests of the owners of an LLP are afforded less protection from the claims of the owners' personal creditors, as compared to the LLC.

Finally, California and New York limit the use of LLPs to professionals, thus eliminating the LLP as a choice for other business owners. (In California, the term "professionals" is defined narrowly to include only lawyers and accountants, further restricting the availability of the LLP there). Since your business entity does not have to be created in the same state in which you reside or do business, it's best to avoid creating an LLP in one of these states.

Warning

Many jurisdictions only offer what is termed a "limited shield" in an LLP. In these states, limited liability protection is significantly reduced. These jurisdictions include:

States Offering Limited-Shield Liability Protection for LLPs

Alaska	Louisiana	Ohio
Arkansas	Maine	Pennsylvania
District of Columbia	Michigan	South Carolina
Hawaii	Nevada	Tennessee
Illinois	New Hampshire	Texas
Kansas	New Jersey	Utah
Kentucky	North Carolina	West Virginia

Other states afford the LLP the same "full shield" protection as that enjoyed in the LLC and corporation. Because the LLP is so relatively new, the law here is rapidly evolving. Expect more states to change the liability shield in the LLP from limited to full.

In addition, in many states, the business interests of the owners of an LLP are afforded less protection from the claims of the owners' *personal* creditors, as compared to the LLC. Specifically, an LLC can be formed in a state that protects the owner's business interest against the claims of his personal creditors. This is not possible with the LLP, as no state affords this protection to LLP owners.

Warning

The small business owner should generally avoid the LLP in "limited shield" states, because it offers less protection from liability there, as compared to either the LLC or the corporation.

There is still one instance when an LLP makes sense: When the business owner is operating a very large, complex general partnership, conversion to an LLP rather than an LLC will be less expensive and less burdensome. Even here, however, it makes sense to form the LLP in a "full shield" state, even if that is not where the business's operations are conducted.

Did You Know?

Where professionals operate in the LLP form, many states impose mandatory insurance requirements on the owners. These requirements are not usually imposed on the owners of an LLC, although this may be an oversight that will be changed in the future.

Starting a Limited Liability Limited Partnership

As if business owners did not have enough choices to make, a new business form—the limited liability limited partnership (LLLP)—is beginning to emerge in the law. An LLLP is a limited partnership that registers under state law so the general partner will have limited liability, similar to the limited partners. This is similar to the process of a general partnership registering to be recognized as a limited liability partnership (LLP), so that *all* of the owners have limited liability.

The LLLP form is primarily used to *convert* an existing limited partnership previously created under state law. However, it will also probably prove popular as an alternative to forming an LLC in those states that allow foreclosure of an owner's business interest, and forced liquidation of the business by the owner's *personal* creditors.

Colorado, Delaware, Florida, Georgia, Maryland and Texas recognize the LLLP. More states are likely to follow suit in the future.

Did You Know?

Because of the availability of entity structures like the limited liability company (LLC), LLP and LLLP, the general partnership and the limited partnership will likely become obsolete in the future. Despite this trend, don't hesitate to use any available entity structure that best meets your particular needs.

CORPORATIONS

One of the best-known and most widely used business entity forms is the corporation. The main advantage of a corporation is the liability protection it provides its owners or shareholders.

Liability is limited because the corporation is a legal entity separate from its shareholder owners. As a separate legal entity, the corporation has a perpetual life and is liable for its own debts, to the extent of the corporation's assets.

The assets of a shareholder are considered personal and cannot be reached by corporate creditors, unless the veil of corporate limited liability is pierced. This can happen when, for example, the required corporate formalities (having annual directors' and shareholders' meetings, etc.) aren't followed, when the corporation has negligible assets of its own, or when the shareholders frequently use corporate assets as if they were personal assets. In effect, the corporate veil could be pierced (by a court when a lawsuit is filed against the corporation and its shareholders) because the corporate form is a mere sham that exists to enable shareholders to avoid personal liability. If this occurs, the shareholders will be liable for the obligations of the corporation.

Warning

Although the corporate form generally results in limited liability, lenders usually require the shareholders of small, closely held corporations to personally guarantee corporate loans. If you personally guarantee the loans, you will have to pay the lender from personal funds if the corporation is unable to pay.

Forming a corporation (also known as a C corporation) is more complicated and more expensive than forming a sole proprietorship or a simple partnership. However, the process is not that difficult. To form a corporation, articles of incorporation must be filed with the secretary of state's office in the state of organization. Upon acceptance, the secretary of state's office will send a certificate of incorporation. Many states require a copy of this certificate be kept in the local recorder's office where the corporation resides.

A corporation does not have to be organized in the state in which it is going to do business. It can be organized in any state. Many corporations organize in states like Delaware or Nevada to take advantage of favorable corporate laws. However, be aware that corporations generally must register and pay an annual fee in every state in which they do business. If you incorporate in a state that's not your home state, you'll be paying fees to an additional state.

A corporation is owned by its shareholders, but they don't have any direct control over the day-to-day operations of the business. The shareholders are responsible for electing directors of the corporation. Then, the directors oversee the business and make major corporate decisions, such as appointing officers. The directors meet at least annually to assess the past performance of the corporation and to plan for the future. Ultimately, the officers of the corporation are responsible for the day-to-day operations of the company.

Once the directors are elected and the corporate officers are appointed, the corporation can begin to operate. However, it is important that the corporation observes all the formalities of being a corporation. These include, among other things, issuing stock certificates to the shareholders, holding annual meetings, recording the minutes of the meetings in the corporate register, and electing directors or ratifying the status of existing directors.

Warning

 In small, closely held corporations, make sure all corporate formalities are observed. If they aren't, someone suing the corporation may be able to show that the corporation is not a separate entity from its shareholders. The shareholders then will be liable for the corporation's debts.

A corporation with two or more shareholders may require the efforts of all of the shareholders to succeed, especially in the early life of the business. If one shareholder withdraws or dies, the existence of the corporation may be threatened. To protect the corporation and the remaining shareholders, consider buy/sell agreements and key person life insurance policies on the shareholders.

A buy/sell agreement specifies how the value of a shareholder's interest will be determined if a shareholder wants to leave the corporation. Having a buy/sell agreement in place minimizes disputes over the company value and facilitates the purchase of the withdrawing shareholder's interest by the corporation or other shareholders.

Key person life insurance is a policy on the life of key members of an organization to provide cash in the event of the death of that person. The beneficiaries of a key person policy are the organization or the organization members. In a corporation, key person life insurance can be purchased on the life of all shareholders or on some designated class such as corporate officers. The life insurance proceeds can be used by the corporation to keep the business going in the absence of the key shareholder or officer. The proceeds also can be used to buy out the deceased shareholder's interest pursuant to a buy/sell agreement.

Statutory Close Corporations

Some states allow a type of corporation called a statutory close corporation, which may appeal to small business owners. This form is one managed by its shareholders. Directors do not have to be elected, and officers do not have to be appointed. Besides eliminating these formalities, the laws usually streamline some of the other meeting and voting requirements. The intent is to relieve some of the administrative burdens to the small corporation owner. If a close corporation appeals to you, consult an attorney to determine the availability of this option.

Warning

Don't confuse a statutory close corporation with the generic term "close corporation." The statutory close corporation is created under a supplemental state corporation statute.

The generic term close corporation is often used to refer to any corporation formed under a state's regular corporation statutes where the stock is not *traded on an exchange, such as the New York Stock Exchange. Calling an entity a close corporation does not mean it is a statutory close corporation. Unless the corporation is created in a state that allows this option, with the required special language in the articles of organization, it will not be a statutory close corporation.*

State statutory close corporation statutes generally require that there be a limited number of shareholders (under 30 or, in some states, under 50), and that certain transfer restrictions appear on the stock certificates. The statutory close corporation must be formed under the special statute with particular language used in the articles of organization. A regular corporation can also be converted to a statutory close corporation in states that allow this type of corporation.

The following jurisdictions recognize the statutory close corporation:

States Allowing Statutory Close Corporations

Alabama	Kansas	South Carolina
Arizona	Maryland	Texas
Delaware	Missouri	Vermont
District of Columbia	Montana	Wisconsin
Georgia	Nevada	Wyoming
Illinois	Pennsylvania	

In addition, California, Maine, Ohio and Rhode Island have provisions within their regular corporation statutes that permit election to statutory close corporation status, but do not have special statutory close corporation statutes.

If your home state does not allow for the creation of a statutory close corporation, you can simply form the entity in one of the above states, and then register it to do business in your home state. When choosing a state, the laws of the state in which the entity is formed will govern its legal affairs. The benefits derived from forming a statutory close corporation in one of these states, and then registering the corporation in the home state, will usually outweigh any additional costs involved.

Professional Corporations

The corporate form also can be used for professional service providers. The main advantage is that members are not liable for the malpractice of others in the corporation, but they still remain liable for their own individual acts. Only professionals can own shares, and the corporation can provide just one form of service (i.e., a professional corporation of lawyers who are also accountants can provide legal services but not accounting services).

The process of incorporation is essentially the same as for any other corporation. However, a professional corporation usually must identify itself as such in its name—although requirements differ, depending on the state (see page 115). There are many other aspects of professional corporations that should be addressed before you venture into this form of entity. Your attorney or accountant can advise you as to whether the professional corporation is right for your situation.

Corporate Tax Issues

Part of the essence of the corporate form is that corporations are separate taxable entities subject to federal and state taxation (except for S corporations, discussed later). Unlike sole proprietorships and partnerships, corporate earnings don't flow directly to the owner or owners, but are taxed at the corporate level. When that after-tax income is passed on to the shareholders as a distribution or dividend, it is taxed again on the shareholder's individual tax return.

Double taxation may be partially or completely avoided in a small business by paying a salary to the employee shareholder, since the salaries, benefits and required payroll taxes are deductible expenses for the corporation. After these expenses are paid, only the remaining earnings are subject to corporate income tax. However, the tax laws governing this area are complex and should be discussed with your accountant or your attorney.

Also, be aware of the tax consequences upon dissolution of a corporation. With all forms of business entity except a C corporation, dissolution and distribution of the business's assets to the owners is, at worst, a single taxable event. In a C corporation, a double tax may be due: The corporation may owe a capital gains tax on liquidation, and the individual shareholders also must recognize a gain upon the transfer of proceeds from the corporate entity to the individual recipient. Consequently, dissolving a C corporation can have serious tax ramifications, so think carefully about incorporating in this form if you anticipate a short-term business opportunity.

Finally, for all corporations, a Federal Employer Identification Number must be obtained by filing a Form SS-4, Application for Employer Identification Number. You may obtain a Form SS-4 by calling the Internal Revenue Service at 1-800-TAX-FORM.

Save Money

If limited liability is not a concern for your business, one strategy you can implement is to begin the business in an unincorporated form, such as a sole proprietorship or partnership, so business losses in the early years of the business can shelter your other income. These "passed through" losses can be used to offset other income you may have. When the business becomes profitable, you can incorporate.

Advantages of a Corporation

- **Earnings can be retained** — The corporation can hold some of its earnings for future investment or dividends; it does not have to pay out all profits to its owners as taxable dividends.

- **Limited liability** — Corporate shareholders are generally not responsible for the debts and obligations of the corporation.

- **Ease of formation** — Forming a corporation is generally a mechanical process dictated by state law.

Disadvantages of a Corporation

- **Formalities required** — A corporation must follow certain formalities dictated by state law to maintain its corporate status.

- **Administration** — The administration of a corporation is complicated because certain federal and state tax procedures are necessary, so therefore certain accounting methods may not be available.

- **Cost** — The cost to incorporate, and pay annual state filing fees, can be considerable. Also, the administrative costs of accounting and tax preparation may be expensive due to the complexity of complying with corporate laws.

S CORPORATIONS

For most purposes, an S corporation is not a separate type of corporation. An S corporation operates in the same manner as a regular (or C) corporation. It must have directors, officers and shareholders who function in the same manner as their regular corporation counterparts.

The difference between these two organizational forms is the S corporation has elected to be federally taxed much like a partnership. After making the S election, the corporation's income, losses, tax credits and other taxable items flow through the corporation to the shareholders. Thus, income is only taxed once, at the shareholder level. If a corporation does not make an S corporation election, corporate income is taxed twice: once at the corporate level and again at the shareholder level when received as a dividend.

At first blush, it seems every corporation should elect S status to eliminate the double taxation of income. However, you should discuss this option with your accountant or attorney because there are disadvantages to making the election and restrictions on who is eligible to make it.

The business must be a domestic corporation with no more than one class of stock. It may not have more than 75 shareholders, and all must agree to S corporation election. All shareholders must be either a living person or an estate or trust that specifically qualifies under the law. No shareholder may be a non-resident alien.

S Corporation Tax Issues

A number of formal requirements must be met in order to achieve S corporation status. Among these is the need to file an election statement with the IRS, signed by all of the shareholders. The timing of this filing is important. We strongly suggest you discuss the tax and compliance implications of S corporation status with your attorney.

Generally speaking, the S corporation elects to be taxed like a partnership for federal tax purposes. After making the S election, the income, losses, tax credits, and other tax items of the corporation flow through the corporation to the shareholders. Thus, income is only taxed once at the shareholder level. If a corporation does not make an S corporation election, corporate income is taxed twice: once at the corporate level and again at the shareholder level when corporate income is distributed as a dividend.

Finally, for all S corporations, a Federal Employer Identification Number must be obtained by filing a Form SS-4, Application for Employer Identification Number. You may obtain a Form SS-4 by calling the Internal Revenue Service at 1-800-TAX-FORM.

Advantages of an S Corporation

- **Cash method of accounting** — Regular corporations must use the accrual method of accounting unless they are considered small corporations (having gross receipts of $5,000,000 or less). However, S corporations usually don't have to use the accrual method unless they have inventory.

- **No personal holding company tax** — An S corporation can accumulate passive income that is then distributed to its shareholders. On the other hand, a corporation with S status can't deduct 70 percent of dividends received, as a C corporation can. However, a C corporation accumulating passive income is at risk of being classified and taxed as a personal holding company, which is a corporation owned by a small number of individuals receiving 60 percent or more of its income in the form of dividends, interest and rents. The income of a personal holding company is taxed at the highest individual tax rate to prevent individuals from forming corporations merely to take advantage of low corporate tax rates.

- **Capital gains** — In an S corporation, capital gains are passed through to the shareholders without having the character of the gain changed. Thus, shareholders can take advantage of the lower maximum tax rate on long-term capital gains (20 percent for property held more than one year). Corporations without S status pass the capital gains to their shareholders as dividends, which are treated as ordinary income. Dividends treated as ordinary income can be taxed at a rate of up to 38.6 percent in 2003 (37.6 percent in 2004 and 2005).

Disadvantages of an S Corporation

- **Limit on number of shareholders** — No more than 75 shareholders are allowed.

- **Limited losses** — Although shareholders of S corporations have the ability to deduct pass-through losses, they may not be able to deduct all the losses allocated to them because such losses are only available to the extent of the shareholder's basis in the S corporation. This tax accounting concept basically limits the amount of losses an S corporation shareholder can take. (However, C corporation shareholders ordinarily can't deduct any losses at all, unless their stock becomes worthless or is sold at a loss).

- **Calendar year** — An S corporation must adopt a calendar year as its tax year, unless it can establish a business purpose for having a fiscal year.

- **One class of stock** — An S corporation can only have one class of stock, which can impair the corporation's ability to raise capital. However, nonvoting stock is not considered a separate class for this purpose.

- **Taxable fringe benefits** — Most fringe benefits provided by the corporation are taxable as compensation to employee-shareholders who own more than 2 percent of the corporation.

LIMITED LIABILITY COMPANIES

A limited liability company (LLC) is a hybrid entity combining the tax flow-through aspects of a partnership with the liability protection of a corporation or a limited partnership. A member of an LLC is protected from personal liability if he manages the business, unlike a limited partner, who becomes personally liable if he assumes management duties. Also, there is no general partner equivalent with unlimited liability, as in a limited partnership arrangement.

Warning

Although the LLC form generally results in limited liability for its members, lenders usually require some or all members of a limited liability company to personally guarantee business loans.

Nevertheless, an LLC provides a great structure when combined with other asset protection strategies. To learn more about such strategies, please consult our book Safe Harbors: An Asset Protection Guide for Small Business Owners, *available at www.toolkit.cch.com or at major book retailers nationwide.*

To form an LLC, articles of organization must be filed with the secretary of state's office. This document contains information about the LLC, such as its name, address, purpose, organizing members, registered agent, etc. In addition, some jurisdictions also require the filing of an operating agreement, which is similar to a partnership agreement. Its purpose is to guide the conduct of the business. If an operating agreement is not required to be filed with the articles of organization, the agreement generally can be in written or oral form. As a precautionary measure, the agreement should always be written, in order to limit future conflicts regarding the terms of the operation.

Warning

A defectively formed LLC or corporation will be deemed a sole proprietorship (if there is one owner) or a general partnership (if there are two or more owners). In either case, the owner or owners will lose their limited liability protection. Instead, they will have unlimited personal liability for all of the entity's debts and for the acts of the business's employees.

Therefore, because of the possible consequences, professional guidance is always a good idea when forming a business entity.

LLC Tax Issues

For federal tax purposes, an LLC is considered a partnership (see page 95). The LLC itself is not taxed. All income or loss is passed to the LLC members and is reported on their individual income tax returns at their own individual tax rates, according to an agreed-upon allocation of interests.

All income must be reported as distributed, whether or not the members actually received their shares, or even if the money is retained in the business as capital. For losses, each member may not deduct an amount in excess of his or her total personal investment.

Even though taxes are paid individually, the LLC is generally required to file a tax return (Form 1065, *U.S. Partnership Return of Income*) reporting income and loss to the IRS, as well as how the distribution was divided among the members (Schedule K-1). If the LLC has only a single owner, the LLC is treated like a sole proprietorship and the owner must simply file a Schedule C with the annual Form 1040.

Finally, for all LLCs, a Federal Employer Identification Number must be obtained by filing a Form SS-4, Application for Employer Identification Number. You may obtain a Form SS-4 by calling the Internal Revenue Service at 1-800-TAX-FORM.

Advantages of a Limited Liability Company

- **Limited liability** — Members are shielded from being personally liable for acts of the LLC and its members. The same cannot be said for a corporation, where a personal creditor with a charging order against the corporation may attach *and* vote a debtor's shares in the corporation in a harmful way (like forcing a liquidation of the business to satisfy the debt if the debtor's interest was a majority interest).

- **Flexible membership** — Individuals, partnerships, trusts or corporations can be participating members.

- **Management** — Members can manage the LLC or elect a group to do so.

- **Flow-through treatment** — Income, losses, deductions and tax credits flow through the LLC to individual members.

- **Privacy** — An LLC may afford its members greater privacy than other forms of organization requiring owners to be identified. However, each jurisdiction has its own specific regulations.

Did You Know?

If you are torn between choosing an S corporation or an LLC entity structure, you should know that LLCs do provide some additional advantages to growing businesses. Like a partnership, an LLC has the ability to make disproportionate distributions to its owners (for example, a LLC member may have a 50 percent ownership interest in LLC assets, but be entitled to 60 percent of the income if the operating agreement so provides).

In contrast, S corporations must generally make all distributions pro-rata in accordance with the number of shares held by each owner. An LLC can have an unlimited number of investors, whereas an S corporation is limited to 75 shareholders.

Disadvantages of a Limited Liability Company

- **Multiple members** — Some jurisdictions do not allow LLCs to have only one member. If this is true in your state, you could obtain limited liability by operating as an S corporation.

- **No free transferability of interests** — Transferability of interests is usually restricted to enable the LLC to be treated as a partnership.

- **LLC status could vary** — Not all jurisdictions have similar LLC statutes.

- **Cost** — An LLC usually costs more to form and maintain than a sole proprietorship or a general partnership. States may also charge an initial formation fee and an annual fee; for more information, check with your secretary of state's office or visit our web site at http://www.toolkit.cch.com.

Part III

Opening For Business

So far, you've done preliminary analyses and made the crucial choices. You've assembled your team of professional help, and you know what kind of business you will launch and how it will be organized. At this point, your pre-opening efforts are entering the final stages.

Now, it's time to get started on actually developing your new business venture into its completed form. From here on out, you'll be taking the physical steps necessary to turn your concept into a thriving business operation.

Don't hurry through these last steps in an effort to get to opening day. This is the chance to take the initiative and set up a business that reflects the individual qualities of its owner. All the activities discussed here offer the opportunity to create a business according to your particular vision.

From establishing your unique business identity to designing your specific plan for success, you will be preparing to make your own mark. Where you work and how you perform the business's necessary functions all reflect the professionalism you are trying to convey to potential customers.

Then, once you have an understanding of these final startup activities, we'll step back and look at the total actual costs involved in getting to this point. Every business owner should keep track of every penny—that should go without saying. But very young businesses especially need to watch the bottom line and try to plan for every contingency. After all, going out of business not long after you open is not a particularly good reflection of your business abilities.

In this third and final part of the book, we'll examine the preparations necessary to better your chances for success as well as how to translate those plans into an efficient business operation.

Chapter 7: Preparing To Succeed outlines a number of ways to secure your business's financial future. You'll need to create an identity, consider your marketing options, design your action plan for business operations and bring all these ideas together in a business plan. There is no set way to do any of these activities—it depends on the individual owner.

Chapter 8: Setting Up Shop provides an overview of what to think about when locating and designing your business facility and everything that goes in it, whether it's a home office or separate office. This includes the physical plant and equipment. Your largest cash outlays will probably be here, so take it upon yourself to explore all options.

Chapter 9: Recruiting and Hiring takes you through the process of staffing your business. We cover the types of help available as well as how to define the position you're looking for. But before you hire the right person, you'll need to understand the legal ramifications of the screening and hiring process. Finally, we'll go through the guidelines, legal and otherwise, for an efficient payroll system.

Chapter 10: Figuring the Cost of Opening Your Doors lets you know how much it's going to take to realize your vision, now that the startup steps are completed. But the cost to start a business doesn't end with your grand opening. You'll also need to budget your startup cash to get through those first few months, when sales are sporadic and cash flow is dry. We'll also show you how to set up an accounting system to keep track of these costs and allow you to work more efficiently with your accountant.

Chapter 7

Preparing To Succeed

In this chapter, we'll look at some of the pre-opening activities that need to be done before literally setting up shop. As a small business owner, you can't underestimate the importance of making the right preparations. Success doesn't just happen; you must plan for it.

The first issue we'll examine is establishing your business's identity. Depending on your organizational form (discussed in the last chapter), you'll have to follow specific rules for registering your business's name. And then we'll show you how to protect that identity as well.

Next, we'll go through some initial marketing considerations for your new business, including analyzing the market, packaging and pricing, and promoting your operation.

Then, we'll discuss designing action plans for your new venture. You'll need to organize your business responsibilities, set up an outline to follow for completing day-to-day operations and try to plan for any contingency—good or bad.

Finally, we'll address business planning. For complete information on how to prepare a business plan that will increase your chances for success, see our companion publication, *Business Plans That Work for Your Small Business*. Here, we'll consider how a business plan fits into the scheme of pre-opening activities.

ESTABLISHING YOUR BUSINESS IDENTITY

You can't underestimate the importance of first impressions, and most people initially may encounter your business through the identity you establish for it. This identity includes the name of your operation, but covers other proprietary items as well, such as any patents, trademarks and logos, and copyrights. After spending all this time and money developing your concept or product, you'll need to take steps to secure your carefully constructed business identity.

Pick and Register a Name

Naming your business may not be as simple as it seems. Try to make the name short, easy to remember, descriptive of the business and capable of drawing attention. Also, it must not mislead or in any way imply something the business is not. For example, you can't lead people to believe your business is a licensed plumbing contractor if you haven't received a plumbing license.

Depending on the business form you choose, you may have to register and receive approval from the local or state government in the jurisdiction where the business is organized. Below are specific rules and requirements for each of the various business entities:

- **Sole proprietorships** — These are presumed to operate under their owner's name. Otherwise, most jurisdictions require a fictitious owner affidavit to be filed, indicating the business operates under an assumed name and identifying the owner.

Work Smart

If you are going to use a name other than your own for your business, contact the county recorder of deeds' office (or government equivalent) that your business will be operating in to get specific information and any necessary forms.

- **General partnerships** — Similar to sole proprietorships, these are presumed to be operating under the names of the partners. If this is not the case, a fictitious owner affidavit is required.

- **Limited partnerships** — The naming process for these businesses involves more formalities. The name has to be registered with the secretary of state's office by filing a certificate of limited partnership, and it must include the words "limited partnership," the letters "L.P." or some other phrase indicating its status. Most statutes specifically identify which descriptions can be used.

Work Smart

A limited partnership's name must be unique. If the name is already in use by another limited partnership, the certificate of limited partnership will be rejected. Save time and effort by determining whether the proposed name is available before filing the certificate.

You can find out the name's availability by calling your secretary of state's office. If the name has been reserved by someone else, they'll tell you.

- **Corporations** — These also require a formal process and a unique name. The name has to be registered with the secretary of state's office, and must not be in use or reserved for another corporation; otherwise, your articles of incorporation will be rejected. You can call the secretary of state's office to find out in advance whether a particular name is available. Or if you have access to certain online services like Lexis/Nexis, a legal research database, you can electronically search your state's database of names to see what's available. Generally, the name must include any of the words "corporation," "incorporated," "limited," "company" or "chartered"; the letters "Inc." or "Corp."; or some other phrase indicating the entity is a corporation. Most state laws specifically identify which descriptions can be used.

Did You Know?

If the corporate name is available, see if the state will let you reserve it. Most states will allow you to reserve a name for a period of time, provided the name isn't already taken.

- **S corporations** — These are subject to the same name rules as regular corporations. S corporations do not have to indicate their status as such in the name. An S corporation's status only has to be identified when filing federal income tax returns and, in some instances, state income tax returns.

- **Professional corporations** — These are generally subject to the same name rules that apply to corporations, with one exception. The name must include the words "professional corporation," the letters "P.C." or some other phrase indicating its status. Most statutes specifically identify which descriptions can be used.

- **Limited liability companies or partnerships**— Again, naming is a formal process. The name has to be reserved with the secretary of state's office, usually when the articles of organization are registered. It also must include the words "limited liability company" or "limited liability partnership," the letters "L.L.C." or "L.L.P.," or some other phrase indicating its status. Most statutes specifically identify which descriptions can be used.

Work Smart

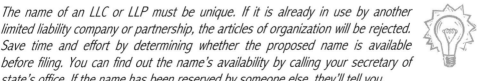

The name of an LLC or LLP must be unique. If it is already in use by another limited liability company or partnership, the articles of organization will be rejected. Save time and effort by determining whether the proposed name is available before filing. You can find out the name's availability by calling your secretary of state's office. If the name has been reserved by someone else, they'll tell you.

Protect Your Ideas

Besides your business's name, other factors make up your operation's unique identity. Very likely, you're going into business because you feel you've developed a product or service that separates you from the pack. Now that you've invented a better mousetrap, and you anticipate people beating a path to your door, you'd be wise to protect your investment.

Patents, trademarks and copyrights are collectively known as intellectual property and generally refer to the rights associated with intangible knowledge or concepts. Intellectual property may be a concern if your business is developing (or has developed) a product, process or concept you are going to market.

Intellectual property also may be a concern if your business is using a process created by someone else, whether you know about it or not. The laws surrounding this subject are quite complicated. If you have any concerns, you should ask your attorney what to do. If some legal work needs to be done, your attorney will probably recommend another lawyer who specializes in this area.

Here's a short description of some of the issues pertaining to patents, trademarks and copyrights, which should help you get a better feel for what they are:

- **Patent** — This is the grant of a right to an inventor by the U.S. government. The right embodied in a patent allows the inventor (or the patent holder, if the patent has been assigned) to exclude others from making or using the invention for a period of time, usually 17 years. Patent searches can be conducted to find out if someone else already has a patent on a product, process or concept you're going to build or market.

- **Trademark** — This is the right to use a specific name, word, phrase, symbol, logo, design, sound, color or a combination of any of these elements to identify your products and distinguish them from others. The name must be sufficiently unique to identify your products; you can't obtain trademark rights to a generic term like "computers" or "coffee." A service mark is similar to a trademark, but refers to the right to use a name to identify the source of services and distinguish that source from other providers. If you have a name or some other item you plan on using as a symbol of your business, it's a good idea to conduct a trademark screen to make certain it isn't already in use. If you have computer access, you can do low-cost, preliminary trademark screens using the "Power Tools" service at the *CCH Business Owner's Toolkit* (http://www.toolkit.cch.com).

- **Copyright** — This is the right to reproduce a certain work if the work is in fixed form. A copyright is secured automatically when the work is created; however, in order to be able to enforce a copyright, the work should be registered with the federal government. A copyright term is for the life of the creator plus 50 years. Penalties for copyright infringement can be avoided by showing the work in question was created independently of the copyrighted work.

INITIAL MARKETING CONSIDERATIONS

As a small business owner, one of your greatest tasks will be to spread the word about your new product or service. Here are some points to think about when you begin to market your new business.

Market Analysis and Planning

As previously mentioned, the marketing plan is a key component of your business's strategy for success. It summarizes the "who, what, where, when and how much" questions of company marketing and sales activities for the planning year:

- **Who** are your target buyers?

- **What** sources of uniqueness or positioning in the market do you have?

- **How** will you communicate that uniqueness to your target buyers?

- **Where** and **when** will you implement your marketing spending plans?

- **How much** sales, spending and profits will you achieve?

Many of these issues were previously addressed in Chapter 2 while discussing the formative stages of picking the right business for you. Now, it's time to come up with a detailed plan and begin executing your ideas. Here are the major elements of any good marketing plan:

- **Situation analysis** — Describes the total marketing environment in which the company competes and the status of company products and distribution channels. Your research should start with the big picture of macroenvironmental influences on your business down through descriptions of the industry, competition, target buyers/end users, product trends and your company's distribution channels.

- **Opportunity and issue analysis** — Analyzes the major *external* opportunities and threats to the company, and the *internal* strengths and weaknesses of the company, along with a discussion of key issues facing the company. External opportunities and threats should be identified with possible programs to capitalize on the opportunities and possible solutions to potential threats. Internal strengths and weaknesses should be examined in a competitive context. Key issues to be addressed are decisions that will be made by the company—based upon the analysis of these external opportunities and threats, and internal company strengths and weaknesses—which help to determine objectives, strategies and tactics.

- **Goals and objectives** — Outlines major company goals, and the marketing and financial objectives. All objectives should be carefully quantified, where possible, especially in terms of an achievable time or date. Objectives also should be reasonable and should include both short- and long-term goals.

- **Marketing strategy** — Provides the company's marketing strategy statement. It should summarize your findings about the key target buyer description, market segments the company will compete in, the unique positioning of the company and its products compared to the competition, the reasons why it is unique or compelling to buyers, price strategy versus the competition, marketing spending strategy with advertising and promotion, and possible R&D and market research expenditure strategies. You may find it useful to keep in mind *the four Ps of marketing* as you define the scope of your marketing strategy.

The Four Ps of Marketing

Product — *What is the good or service your business will offer? How is that product better than those against which it will compete? Why will people buy it?*

Price — *How much can you charge? How do you balance between sales volume and price to maximize income?*

Promotion — *How will your product or service be positioned in the marketplace? Will your product carry a premium image with a price to match? Will it be an inexpensive, no-frills alternative to similar offerings from other businesses? What kinds of advertising and packaging will you use?*

Place — *Which sales channels will you use? Will you sell by telephone, or will your product be carried in retail outlets? Which channel will economically reach your market?*

- **Sales and marketing plan** — Outlines each specific marketing event designed to increase sales. This plan will generally cover a calendar year, broken down by month or by quarter. For example, it may contain a summary of quarterly promotional and advertising plans, with spending, timing, and share or shipment goals for each program. Naturally, sales and marketing plans should be a logical outgrowth of short- and long-term company objectives as well as your marketing strategy.

Positioning Your Business

To develop the proper strategy for your business, you must understand what separates your product from that of your competitors. Then, more importantly, what do these differences mean to the target buyers? Positioning is the perceived value of these differences, and your goal is to effectively communicate the importance of your uniqueness to those most interested in buying your offerings.

In some cases, there may be little or no difference between your product and others. Or the differences may be very difficult to communicate (think of the difference between Coke and Pepsi). The challenge here is to create some differences through your positioning, and then use that identity to influence buyers.

Example

Joe's Redhots will sell premium-quality hot dogs and other ready-to-eat luncheon products to upscale businesspeople in high-traffic urban locations. Joe's Redhots will be positioned versus other street vendors as the "best place to have a quick lunch." This is because Joe's Redhots has the cleanest carts; the most hygienic servers; the purest, freshest products; and the best values. Prices will be at a slight premium to reflect this superior vending service. Joe's Redhots will also be known for its fun and promotional personality, offering consumers something special every week.

Setting a Budget

Spending on marketing support may range from less than 1 percent of net sales for industrial business-to-business operations to 10 percent or more for companies selling packaged consumer goods. Many small businesses estimate revenues, subtract expenses and use whatever is left for marketing support. A more rational approach would be to estimate what your competitors spend and then try to match it. If you are new to the marketplace, you may have to be more aggressive to establish your operation.

Packaging

Packaging represents a very concrete way to communicate with your target market and express the positioning of your business. People often will get to know your product or service, at least initially, by the manner in which it is presented. And this includes the look and the cost of what you're providing.

Package design is more than just the appearance of the physical wrapper or outer container that a product comes in. Packaging can be the way in which services are bundled together for an intermediate buyer or end user. In this case, packaging can be a collection of logo identifications on clothing, uniforms, tools, stationery, forms, hang tags and other paraphernalia. Packaging can also be the unique style in which a company provides its services.

For physical products, the preceding still applies. Moreover, the package label or wrapper may represent the product's entire business positioning, list of features and benefits, advertising and promotion—especially for smaller businesses. Package design essentials apply to both service and physical product companies, and must do all of the following:

- **Reflect the business's positioning or unique values** — Are you trying to convey a high-end image through elaborate or expensive packaging, or are you offering a low-cost alternative that could be immediately recognizable through a more simple approach?

- **Communicate graphic identity** — Do you have a symbol or logo that people will notice and associate with your business?

- **Reflect target buyer values** — Are your end users' demographics, lifestyle, activities and interests reflected in your packaging presentation, thereby increasing product appeal?

Pricing

Pricing must reflect not only your costs to produce the product or service at the expected volume, but also the value your customers place on what you offer. What's more, price is a way to differentiate your business from others, especially in the consumer market.

The ideal price for any product or service is one that is acceptable to both buyer and seller. From the buyer's standpoint, the right price is a function of product purchase value and other competitive choices in the marketplace. From the seller's viewpoint, there are many potential pricing objectives. But the basic concern for almost all small businesses is to price products to maximize both sales and profits, while providing enough margin to take care of applicable marketing and overhead expenses.

The following steps are recommended for determination of product pricing for any size business:

- **Analyze the size and composition of your target market** — You must estimate approximately how large your potential sales volume could be, based on a reasonable assessment of your potential market share in the product category, at different price levels.

- **Research price elasticity for your product** — If demand for your product or service changes significantly with slight changes in price, the product category is considered to be *elastic* with respect to price. The greater the price elasticity, the closer you should price your products to similar competitive products, and vice versa.

Example

Grocery store items are often very price sensitive, with +/- 10 percent price changes resulting in significant share and volume changes per brand.

Gourmet food categories are often inelastic. It may require a price increase or decrease of 50 percent to create any perceptible changes in consumers' behavior. Consumers shopping these premium-priced categories are not as value-conscious as shoppers in a regular grocery store environment.

- **Evaluate your product's uniqueness** — The closer your product resembles competitive products, the smaller the price differences that buyers will tolerate, leading to brand-switching when products go on sale. Still, product uniqueness does not guarantee a significant price premium over a competitive product, if the differences aren't recognizable and meaningful to consumers.

- **Select your channels of distribution** — When you have limited resources, it's often best to select a single distribution channel or a limited number of channels that offer the greatest ease of entry against the competition, the lowest costs of entry compared to the competition, the least financial risk and commitment to the trade, sufficient volume potential to reach short-term company goals, and pricing levels to provide acceptable company revenues and profit margins.

- **Consider product life cycles** — Many product categories have significant evolution and life cycles that may affect pricing decisions. For example, with personal computers and software, it now takes as little as six to twelve months before new technology and products are introduced. As a result, pricing cycles also have accelerated to match, with introductory pricing decreasing to significantly lower levels only six to eight months later.

- **Analyze your costs and overhead** — Several objectives need to be addressed in determining correct product pricing: cover the cost of producing the goods or services, cover marketing and overhead expenses, provide profit objectives, afford distribution margin discounts and sales commissions, and be competitive.

Example

A breakeven analysis is a commonly used method that focuses on the volume of sales at which total revenues will equal total costs. The idea is to set the price of a unit of product or service at a level where it will cover all of its own variable costs (material, labor, marketing, etc.) plus its portion of the fixed costs of the company (overhead). At the point where enough units have been sold to cover all fixed and variable costs, breakeven is achieved. After that point, the sales price of a unit sold minus the variable (direct) cost to produce it equals pure profit.

For example, a case of tea beverages in 12-ounce ready-to-drink bottles has a cost of goods of $3.82 per case of 12. Factory price to distributors is $6.54/case. Gross margin (price minus cost of goods) is $2.72/case. If the company's fixed costs (e.g., overhead, factory expenses, etc.) are estimated at $75,000 per year, then the breakeven point would be 27,573.5 cases of tea ($75,000 divided by $2.72/case).

- **Estimate sales at different prices** — The probability of significant sales volume differences at different prices depends upon the price elasticity of the market as well as the number of similar competitors and their perceived quality. The length of time various brands have been on the market, their relative market share, brand loyalty factors, advertising and promotion spending levels, sales support, merchandising efforts, and distribution penetration levels all have an influence on the pricing versus volume equation.

- **Consider secondary pricing strategies** — A company can have many different pricing objectives and strategies. Some businesses may utilize product pricing to attack or defend against a competitor. Also, you'll want to consider these variables when formulating your pricing strategy: discounts for prompt cash payment or quantity purchases, special pricing for seasonal items, senior citizen and student discounts, and promotional incentives to motivate your dealers.

Maxwell House Coffee introduced a second, low-priced brand into their own dominant Eastern United States markets during the 1970s to slow and confuse the introduction of Folger's Coffee into their markets. This new product was packaged and designed to resemble Folger's familiar red can, with pricing set below Folger's Coffee. The new temporary product clogged grocer shelves and made it more difficult and expensive for Folger's to introduce their coffee into new Eastern markets.

- **Select final pricing levels** — These should have flexibility for both increases and discounts to customers. Price increases may be inevitable because of component, ingredient and processing cost increases; the market may or may not absorb these price increases without decreasing volume. Price decreases due to buyer volume and promotional discounts cannot always be planned for. When in doubt, price on the high side, if possible. It's always easier to discount prices than to raise them.

Example

For many years, the overall coffee market volume remained steady in the United States, despite several price increases. However, once ground coffee retail prices went over $4.00 per pound during the 1980s, market volume began to decline rapidly as people switched to tea or alternative beverages. The introduction of espresso bars and specialty blends of coffee during the last 10 years has helped to reverse this decline, despite continued higher prices. Now, better grades of coffee and flavors are being enjoyed by American consumers.

Promotion, Advertising and Public Relations

In order for your business to succeed, you generally need to promote your products or services to the same buyers your competitors are targeting. Even if your business is one-of-a-kind, you still need to tell target buyers your business exists by using some kind of marketing communications. The best way to begin is to construct a positioning statement for your business, expressing the key points you'll include in all promotion, advertising and PR programs.

Promotional programs or advertising are popular ways to spread the word about your product or service. Designed, approved and paid for by the business itself, these activities are direct efforts by you to notify target buyers or end users of your availability in the marketplace.

Public relations (PR) activities are another way to promote the image or reputation of your product. PR is similar to promotion and advertising, but is more indirect, since some or all of the publicity a company's products and services receive from public relations activities may not be controlled by the company.

Executing Your Game Plan

Whatever type of business you're opening, you'll need to create a comprehensive promotional game plan to communicate with your target buyers. Most businesses find they need all three components of marketing communications in some combination. You should narrow down the available choices and build a communications program that makes sense by identifying your target buyer, determining what is meaningfully unique about the product, constructing a business positioning statement, communicating the most meaningful message regarding your unique selling proposition, and setting a reasonable budget for these costs.

Advertising Checklist

❏ ***Communicate a simple, single message.*** *People have trouble remembering someone's name, let alone a complicated ad message. For print ads, the simpler the headline, the better. And every ad element should support the headline message, whether that message is "price," "selection," "quality" or any other concept.*

❏ ***Stick with a likable style.*** *Ads have personality and style. Find a likable style and personality, and stay with it for at least a year, to avoid confusing buyers.*

❏ ***Be credible.*** *If you say your quality or value is the "best" and it clearly is not, advertising will speed your demise, not increase your business. Identifying and denigrating the competition also should be avoided. It is potentially confusing and distracting, and may backfire on you by making buyers more loyal to competitors.*

❏ ***Ask for the sale.*** *Provide easily visible information in the ad for potential customers: location, telephone number, store hours, charge cards accepted.*

❏ ***Make sure the ad looks professional.*** *If you have the time and talent, computer graphics and desktop publishing software can provide professional-looking templates to create good-looking print ads. Consider obtaining writing, artistic and graphics help from local agencies or art studios that have experienced professionals on staff, with expensive and creative computer software in-house. Electronic ads (e.g., TV, radio, Internet) and outdoor ads are best left for professionals to produce.*

❏ ***Be truthful.*** *Whatever advertising medium you select, make sure your message is ethical and truthful. There are stringent laws regarding deceptive practices and false advertising.*

If you're a big manufacturer of business-to-business goods, you may need to do much more personal sales promotion (to purchasing agents of your customer firms) than a consumer goods retailer, who would go to a marketing mix that emphasizes paid advertising.

- **Promotions** — These are opportunities for materials or events that involve direct purchase incentives, as opposed to most advertising, which provides reasons to buy your product instead of the competing brand. Typical promotional activities include games and contests, premiums and gifts, coupons and rebates, and product or service demonstrations. Many small businesses are local or regional, so some promotional activities will be too expensive or inappropriate for the type of goods and services offered. The most important thing is to come up with a promotion that is unique and that sends the right message about your business. And it is critical to monitor the effectiveness of your promotions. If they don't generate results, they aren't worth the time or money you'll spend.

Example

Your gourmet coffee shop ordinarily sells 500 pounds of coffee in an average week. You decide to try a promotion using a coupon, good for 20 percent off the price of coffee purchased during a particular week.

If coffee sales increase enough so the additional sales make up for the lower profit margin, coupons might be a good approach. But if you only sell the same 500 or so pounds to your regular customers, then the coupons are just reducing your profit without providing a reasonable benefit.

- **Advertising** — These impersonal, usually paid communications are intended to inform, educate, persuade and remind. To be successful, they must work in conjunction with other marketing tools and business elements. Also, good advertising must be credible, unique and memorable in order to work. But don't overlook the most effective type of this communication—word-of-mouth advertising. This passes product information to many other potential buyers (and may even include promotional trial demonstrations and free sampling) *at little or no cost to the business.* Satisfied customers are, by far, your best advertisements.

Example

In some respects, typical media advertising (e.g., the Miller Lite "less filling/great taste" ads) acts only as a catalyst to achieve word-of-mouth advertising and increased sales. Successful advertising will achieve many times more ad mentions through word-of-mouth than the number of paid media presentations of the ads.

Low- and No-Cost Advertising

- *Print attractive and informative business cards that include your logo and hand them out everywhere, consistently! If you use letterhead stationery in your business, have it match your business card. Keep your identity as consistent as possible.*

- *Print up some gift certificates. These let your customers introduce you to new customers. Since you get paid up front for the product or service, they are good for your cash flow.*

- *Brochures let you provide a lot of detail about your product or service. Simple three-fold brochure stock may be purchased in small quantities from mail-order suppliers such as Paper Direct (call 1-800-272-7377).*

- *Flyers can be created very inexpensively on your computer or by a local print shop. You can make them as colorful as you like, by using a color printer or old-fashioned colored paper stock. They can be used as bag stuffers or inserts to include with billings.*

- *Doorhangers are very effective and widely used by fast food, home delivery and service businesses. If you choose this medium, use heavy stock so it won't blow off doorknobs and litter the neighborhood.*

- *Inserted ads include mailbox inserts and free-standing inserts. The science behind the mass distribution of inserts is beyond the scope of our discussion here. If you think that inserts could successfully reach your market, call one of the big distributors and learn how much it would cost you to try this kind of program. The industry leaders are ADVO (call 860-285-6100 and they'll give you the local contact, or visit their web site at www.advo.com) and Val-Pak, which is so big that you can find it under "V" in most local phone books (or call them at 1-800-661-0964).*

- *Paper or plastic bags and packaging make economical billboards. Print your name, logo and message on anything you can, and put it on all sides of the packaging. Mailing labels are another perfect medium. Everyone who handles your mail will see your ad at no cost to you.*

- **Public relations** — PR efforts can help to build business and product awareness among target buyers and end users, often at a fraction of the cost of advertising. PR can be an effective way to generate valuable word-of-mouth advertising, sometimes due to the greater credibility and availability of information provided in editorial articles and interviews with your company personnel. Also, public relations is an ongoing process and must be worked at every day on every level of your business, from the way you deal with your employees to how quickly you shovel the snow from in front of your establishment.

Public Relations Ideas

Press releases *— If you make them newsworthy, these can lead not only to great free publicity, but to valuable reprints you can use in your ad efforts. For example, a simple story (and perhaps product examples) about the company's background, founders and products can be written and sent to editors of local newspapers, magazines, TV and radio stations. If the subject is of sufficient interest to the editors, they may call to interview and run a free editorial story reaching thousands or millions of people.*

Public service activities *— These are a fine way to achieve good public relations and free publicity of the best kind. Participate in service clubs such as Rotary and Lions, and join the Chamber of Commerce. Offer to be a speaker at schools or senior centers. Donate your goods or services to local schools or churches, to be given away as raffle or silent auction prizes. Sponsor a little league team.*

Grand openings (or re-openings) *— These are always attention-getters, as are anniversary sales and seasonal promotions. A small business can host open house events, explaining and demonstrating products and services to invited target buyers.*

DESIGNING YOUR ACTION PLANS

Action plans set out the framework by which you will operate and manage your business, in areas not covered by the marketing plan. It covers activities such as hiring and managing employees, obtaining and working with vendors for needed materials and supplies, ensuring production takes place as planned, fulfilling orders, making collections, providing customer service and support after the sale, and dealing with unexpected occurrences or changing conditions. These issues can be conveniently grouped into three categories: operations, management and contingency plans.

Operations Plan

Of the three, planning operations will probably be the most time-consuming. Here is where you detail the necessary steps of how you will create and deliver your product or service. Often, it helps to visualize your business as if it were a linear process that begins with raw materials and ends with a delivery to a satisfied customer. You'll probably be surprised by the number of steps, and how critical the timing and duration are for each step. This planning will be of vital importance when it comes time to set up your business space (see Chapter 8).

While it's easy to relate to production issues in a manufacturing or product-fabricating environment, the concept is also applicable to other types of businesses.

Example

As a consultant, you are engaged to help a company convert from paper-based billing to a computer-based system. The end "product" that you will deliver is assistance in selecting the appropriate software and hardware, training on that new equipment, and supervision of the process by which the data is converted to electronic format. You can do a great job without "producing" anything tangible beyond, perhaps, documentation of the process.

This doesn't mean that you can ignore "production." Consider all the work that you would have to do. First, a working knowledge of the client's existing system has to be acquired. Software and hardware combinations have to be evaluated in light of the client's needs and budget. A conversion process has to be developed so that those portions of the existing data that carry over to the new system are available in the new format. Then, documentation must be prepared to train the client's employees in using the new system. Whether you realized it or not, each of these activities would be part of your production process.

Another production issue you may have to consider is that there may be situations in which completing the job requires work outside your expertise. You must consider all aspects of satisfactorily delivering your product or service, including the acquisition of additional skills or expertise.

Example

A self-employed plumber deals primarily in pipes, faucets and fixtures. Those pipes have a nasty habit of being inside walls, and when the plumbing goes bad, the walls frequently stand between the plumber and the pipe. A good plumber knows that the production process goes beyond his or her primary area of expertise and will plan for the time and costs associated with the non-plumbing activities, such as plastering, required to satisfy customers.

Management Plan

As we've already discussed, a small business owner has to wear many hats while operating the business. These activities include managing any employees you have, as well as performing the back office and administrative duties required to keep the business running.

It's very easy to overlook or underestimate these activities, because many of them aren't directly involved in the tangible production of your product or service, but they are key to your business's survival. Keeping everything on schedule requires you to monitor all the diverse activities and actively intervene when things aren't going according to plan. Set up a process for getting these things done, and secure outside help for those activities that present a major drain on your time and resources.

Contingency Plan

No matter how carefully you prepare, "Murphy's Law" will surely intervene. A contingency plan is an attempt to avoid the disruption of your operation when market or economic conditions change beyond what you're prepared to handle without major adjustments to your business. When planning for the unexpected, it may help to think about the kinds of changes that would have the greatest impact on your business.

Example

Let's say that your business plans to obtain a line of credit, and you negotiate an interest rate of prime plus 2 percent. You estimate that the rate you'll pay is 9 percent, but you can live with a rate as high as 12 percent. Obviously, anything below 9 percent makes it that much easier to meet your planned goals. But what happens if the rate goes to 14 percent or even 20 percent? It happened in the early 1980s, and the change happened over a relatively short period of time. What would you do?

But remember, contingencies don't always involve things going worse than expected.

Example

Assume that your initial marketing plan calls for a mass mailing to 1,000 prospective customers. Assume further that a primary selling point is the immediacy of the need for the customers to act. You expect to get perhaps 10 to 20 paying customers out of the mailing. Instead, you get 243. What do you do? You've sold the market on the need to act quickly, but your business isn't prepared to handle that many customers in the time frame required. If you have a contingency plan, you're ready to act. In this example, it may involve bringing in temporary help, outsourcing certain tasks, or even asking competitors to do the work on a contract basis.

Ultimately, you can only go so far in contingency planning. What's important is that you've identified those areas in which your business is vulnerable to variable factors. If you have already considered possible responses to changes in the market, you will be able to react much more quickly than if you had never even thought of the consequences. So, whether things go better or worse than expected, you will have already identified the likely causes and considered your responses.

DEVELOPING A BUSINESS PLAN

All of the preceding information in this chapter is of vital importance to a brand-new operation. If these issues aren't carefully considered by a prospective business owner, the new venture stands little chance of success. Moreover, the consideration of these issues, and others, make up the content of a formal document called a business plan.

As a practical matter, you'll need a business plan when it comes time to seek almost any kind of financing for your new business. We've devoted an entire book, with five sample plans, to the topic of how to write an effective business plan. We strongly suggest you review the material on business plans, either in our companion book, *Business Plans That Work for Your Small Business,* or at our website www.toolkit.cch.com. For our purposes, we'll examine the business planning process in more general terms.

Business Plan Defined

A key factor in the success of many small businesses has been the existence of a formal, well-thought-out business plan. And without question, most small businesses that succeed in obtaining financing have a formal plan presented to prospective lenders or investors. But a business plan is far more than a formal requirement for getting a loan from a traditional lender.

At its best, a business plan is a detailed blueprint of exactly how your new business is going to go about its fundamental activity—making a profit. Such a blueprint helps you to avoid surprises as you proceed toward the opening of your new business. Unfortunately, most surprises you're likely to encounter will involve taking care of issues you didn't even think about.

The structure provided by a written plan can make it more likely you'll consider all significant factors and let nothing important slip through the cracks. In short, it increases your chances for success. The planning process is an excellent way of evaluating an idea before committing time and money to it. A good plan also establishes a timetable for the completion of activities essential to getting the business up and running.

Contents of a Business Plan

With limited exceptions, there is no set format or order of presentation, because a plan is highly business-specific. For example, issues relating to location can be a key factor for a retail business serving a local market, so these would be given much attention in a business plan. Location would be much less of a factor for a mail-order business serving a national customer base, so a business plan for this operation would place little emphasis on location.

However, regardless of the type of business, most business plans will address the same issues. The order of presentation should be based on the characteristics of the particular business and the uses to which the plan will be put. A plan used to inform employees about how the business will be run should have a different focus than a plan prepared for submission to a bank in an effort to get financing. For someone just getting started, it pays to write a plan just to get your thoughts down on paper in an organized fashion, as a reality check.

Work Smart

If you're one of those people who has difficulty writing, there are many sources of assistance. There are business consultants who can help you write a plan, or review and edit one you've written. Many accountants also have experience writing plans for clients. Particularly if you're writing a plan to obtain financing, you might consider getting some help in making sure your plan looks professional and accurately portrays how you'll turn your business idea into a profitable venture.

Customarily, a business plan has specific elements or sections. The following discussion identifies and describes each of the elements that will make up your plan. They are presented in the order in which they *usually* appear in a plan. Don't feel constrained to follow this exact format if another way makes more sense because of the nature of your business idea. The finished plan should look professional and be concise. In most cases, a business plan won't exceed 20 to 30 pages.

- **Cover page** — Identifies you and your business, and dates the plan. If you've spent any time and effort on a company logo, slogan, or other identifying graphic or text, this is the place to highlight it. Identification information should also be included here.

- **Table of contents** — Makes it easy for readers to find particular information within the plan. If your table of contents runs more than one page in a reasonably sized typeface, your plan is probably too long.

- **Executive summary** — Arguably the single most important part of your business plan. It provides a high-level overview of the entire plan emphasizing the factors you believe will lead to success. It should also state the business's mission. A mission statement is a measurable, definable and actionable project outline explaining your business's purpose for existing.

- **Business background** — Gives information about the business's organization and history (if any), and identifies the product or service the business will provide. Typically, the unique features and benefits of the product or service are highlighted. For a wholly new business, this section will include information about your personal background and skills as they relate to the activities your business will perform. You're trying to give the reader a feel for the flavor of, and make a sales pitch for, the business. It will also contain information about where you intend to locate your business, whether or not you'll be hiring employees, and what type of business entity you've selected.

- **Marketing plan** — Presents an analysis of the market conditions the business will face, sets forth the marketing strategy the business will follow and provides a detailed schedule of the marketing activities the business will use to support sales.

- **Action plans** — Show how operational and management issues will be resolved, including contingency planning. This part of the plan will summarize how you'll create and deliver your product or service. Remember, you may find it useful to think of your business as a linear process beginning with raw materials and ending with a satisfied customer. It also explains how you will manage the administrative duties required to keep the business running. Finally, contingency plans outline your course of conduct if factors affecting your business plan don't turn out as expected.

- **Financial statements and projections** — Demonstrate how the business can be expected to perform financially if the business plan's assumptions are sound. These projections (and any historical information if you have it) include projected profit and loss statements, projected cash flow budgets, and any startup financial information. As a new business owner, you're going to have to be able to sell yourself as a potentially successful business owner. This means including personal financial information that details the amount and source of funds available to invest in the business.

- **Appendix** — Presents supporting documents, statistical analysis, product marketing materials, resumes of key employees, etc. This is the place to put the information that supports the decisions reflected in the plan.

Chapter 8

Setting Up Shop

After much planning and preparation, the time has come for you to put together a facility to house your new business. This entails much more than finding the right building and location. You may have to fill it with equipment and supplies. And possibly remodel it. Don't forget to secure the proper permits and licenses as well.

Also, will customers and suppliers find your operation convenient? Are you fighting established competition? Is there room to grow? And these questions only scratch the surface. As you can see, there is a lot to think about when setting up your physical operation.

In some cases, your facility needs will be such that you'll have to lease office space. In other cases, your facility needs may be minimal and you can work from home. If you have a choice, and all things are otherwise equal, you should probably work from home, primarily because (1) it's a lot cheaper than renting office space and (2) you have less to lose if your business fails. However you envision your ideal facility, as a business owner your vital concern is to make sure it contributes to your profitability, rather than detracting from it.

In this chapter, we'll help you analyze your specific business facility needs and give you some tips on looking for a site. Then, we'll go through the various considerations for a small business owner when setting up and equipping a new location. Ultimately, your search will go much smoother if you know what you want (and need) before you go looking for it.

BUSINESS FACILITIES INSIDE THE HOME

If you're thinking of starting a home-based business, you have a special set of issues to consider, along with all the usual issues that must be faced by anyone who is starting a business.

While working at home can provide you with a freedom from structure not possible in a traditional work setting, it can also result in loneliness and lack of concentration. However, if you make a conscious effort, these common pitfalls can be overcome:

- Are you disciplined enough to work at home? Can you focus on the work that has to be done or will you be tempted to do other things around the house?

- Will you be distracted by family and friends while at home?

- Will customers come to your business? If so, will the customers object to coming to your home rather than a business location? Is there sufficient parking available?

- Will you need employees? Is there adequate space for more than one person to work? Is there sufficient parking available?

- What are the zoning restrictions, if any, that apply to your home? Are home offices prohibited?

- Will the home office income tax deduction be available to you? The criteria for this deduction are very specific. For more information, call the IRS at 1-800-TAX-FORM (1-800-829-3676) and ask for their free Publication 587, *Business Use of Your Home.*

- Can you afford to lease an office at the outset of your business? Working at home could be much less costly.

Work Smart

Try these hints to avoid feeling isolated, and to make and maintain new business contacts:

- *Join professional groups such as industry organizations or associations.*

- *Take classes in areas pertinent to your business and of interest to you.*

- *Participate in and plan events involving people in the business community.*

- *Keep an eye open for contacts and interaction wherever you are—the health club, the supermarket or the neighborhood block party.*

Working at home also can make it difficult to focus on your work. There are many distractions that don't exist in a traditional workplace: chores, errands and guilty pleasures such as watching TV or going to the park. We have a few suggestions for staying focused:

- **Set up a routine to get yourself on task immediately** — For example, upon entering the work area, you could close the door and fire up your computer as a mental cue to begin work.

- **Get organized** — It's also a good idea to have a daily list of goals, or at least one task, to attack as soon as you enter the work area.

- **Plan for distraction** — Despite all plans to the contrary, recognize that distractions are inevitable when you work at home. Even a traditional work setting has its own distractions. To deal with the inevitable distractions, work them into your schedule where you can.

Example

Jason starts work in his home office each day at 10:00 a.m. Every day, his mail is delivered at 12:30 p.m. The mail carrier usually has packages and certified letters that must be signed for, and Jason finds it hard to get right back to work after this daily interruption. To avoid this problem, Jason takes his lunch break every day at 12:30.

Organizing a Home Office

The area of your home where you operate your business—your workplace—will have an impact on the success of your business venture. To make sure this impact is positive, organize it into an efficient tool of your business. Your workplace should encourage productivity when you deal with customers or clients, suppliers, family, friends and neighbors.

The two main goals in creating a workspace are functionality and low cost. Your home office work area should allow you to perform all necessary duties of your business without unduly disrupting the functioning of the rest of your household, and should do so at a cost that doesn't put your new business too deeply in the hole.

- **Define your work area** — Most people working out of their homes find it helpful to have the work area somewhat isolated from the personal areas of the home, particularly if clients and customers will be coming into the work area. If feasible, a separate entrance (or even a detached building on your property) for the work area might be best. A traditional work setting contains natural boundaries for the people in your personal life. However, when you work at home, you will need to create these boundaries so your business, as well as your personal life, can run smoothly and successfully.

- **Watch the cost** — Maybe you've picked a spot for your work area and now are thinking that physical changes should be made to enhance its efficiency (new walls, wood paneling, soundproofing, carpeting, etc.). All of these may be good ideas—and possibly some or all of these changes should be made—but the question is, when? If you are just starting your home business, economy and efficiency should be your watchwords. If you qualify, Uncle Sam may partially subsidize your home office in the form of income tax write-offs. Talk to your accountant about this possibility.

- **Carefully design your workspace** — If you bring customers or other people into your home work area, you should consider whether your desk, furnishings and other equipment convey the right impression. Although these items usually don't have to be expensive or elegant, they may detract from your business image if they are battered or appear unbusinesslike. Your office equipment should convey the impression you are serious (but not stodgy!) about your business, and you are able and willing to provide your customers with superior products or services.

- **Safety concerns** — Your business visitors may not think to look for hazards that are a part of the home, but are not usually encountered in the workplace. If possible, try to keep your visitors out of the personal areas of the house where the belongings of family members may create problems (such as the skateboard at the bottom of the steps). Likewise, aggressive dogs or other animals should be kept away from visitors. Regardless of how hard you try to keep your business area safe for visitors, you should always have adequate liability insurance. (See the discussion of insurance in Chapter 4.)

Work Smart

When people try to interrupt you while you're working, whether it's in person or on the telephone, tactfully let them know you can't be disturbed because you're working on something, you're on a business call, you're with an employee or you're in a meeting. Then let them know when you will be available and make sure it's outside your regular business hours. It may take some time, but your neighbors, friends and family will learn to take your home business as seriously as you do!

Regulatory Matters

If your workplace is also your home, local zoning rules may affect you. While some localities have no zoning laws related to working at home, cities and towns that do have zoning laws usually prohibit or restrict working at home. The main rationale behind these prohibitive or restrictive laws is to maintain the residential character of a neighborhood. On the flip side, it is often illegal to live in some commercially zoned areas where you are running a business.

Local zoning laws can impose many restrictions affecting your ability to maintain a home office or business. Some localities restrict the right of property owners to build separate structures. There also may be restrictions on how much of your home can be used exclusively for your home office or business. Local zoning laws can limit the number of employees you are allowed to have, or prevent you from having any employees working in your home (other than domestics).

Zoning ordinances may also affect your ability to advertise or run your business. For example, some local laws prohibit advertising signage to maintain the residential character of neighborhoods. Many communities also have parking restrictions that could seriously impact your ability to conduct business. Restrictions on the amount and type of vehicular traffic in residential areas also can be an issue.

Zoning rules also may impose environmental restrictions or prohibitions on home businesses. Noise, smoke and odor can all be subject to zoning rules. Certain types of equipment are prohibited due to environmental concerns. The use and disposal of chemicals, hazardous substances, etc., also may be regulated by zoning. These restrictions may prevent you from operating certain businesses in your home.

Finally, depending on your local laws, you may need a home-occupation permit or a business license to have a home office or business. The cost is usually a flat fee or a percentage of annual receipts from your business.

One way to get information is through your local planning department or zoning board, located in your county offices or city hall. Also, if you live in an apartment building, we suggest you contact the manager or board responsible for setting up rules for activities in the building. Similarly, find out if your neighborhood has a homeowner's association and check its policy on businesses run out of the home.

If you live in a condominium or co-op, check the lease or ownership agreement to find out if running a business out of your home is prohibited. If you rent your house or apartment rather than own it, check your lease agreement because it might prohibit a home business operation.

Work Smart

Every public library should contain a copy of the local ordinances, including zoning rules. You can pore over these at your leisure, without alerting any officials about your home-business plans.

Also, you may be able to get information about zoning from local non-government sources such as the Chamber of Commerce, industry associations and trade groups.

BUSINESS FACILITIES OUTSIDE THE HOME

Obviously, a separate outside facility for your business will require a whole additional set of variables to consider. If you're just starting out in business and selecting your first facility, spend some time to consider what you need. This process will require a lot of cold, hard planning, as well as some measure of dreaming. (If you didn't have a little dreamer in you, you probably wouldn't be an entrepreneur!)

On the other hand, if you've been working in your chosen industry for some time as an employee or manager, and are now considering a facility to house your new business, you may have a good idea about what you need. In this case, you may be ready to choose the right facility.

Finally, maybe you have a clear picture of your facility needs and have identified one or more potential sites for your business. Often, the next question is rent or buy? Because important, and complex, tax and cash management issues are tied up in this rent-or-buy question, many small business owners rely heavily on the advice of their accountant or attorney when making this decision. You also may wish to do so. But even if you do, you should be aware this decision will, down the road, influence other business decisions that go beyond tax and cash management issues.

Determining Your Facility Needs

When you visualize the ideal facility for your business, your thoughts may run along several lines. You may first think of the interior layout: the amount of space, how it would be subdivided into rooms or work areas to best serve you, and how it could be constructed or decorated to provide the capabilities and business atmosphere best suiting your operation. Or you may envision its exterior: its appearance (and that of surrounding buildings) and the impression it conveys about your business, its location (on well-traveled streets or tucked away in the country), and its provision for necessary features such as parking facilities and loading docks.

Possibly you first think about the community in which you'll locate your business. Will it be in a large city, in a suburb, in a small town or in a remote wilderness area? Will its location provide necessities such as a trained workforce, or convenient access to a major airport or other transportation facilities? Can you locate it anywhere, or will you count on a particular location to make a statement about your business?

Or maybe a bad experience with a previous or current facility makes you think along the lines of what to avoid: poor business location, inadequate building space or substandard transportation access for customers, suppliers or employees.

If you are just getting into business, these decisions surrounding the choice of a business facility can be particularly worrisome. Where do you start? Do you first pick the community in which you wish to locate the business, amassing all the information on it? Should you look at prospective sites and buildings, and imagine how well your business would operate in each? Should you look around for geographic areas not well served by potential competitors, then concentrate on those unmet needs?

These and many more inquiries deserve consideration as you search out a business facility. But, particularly if this is the first time you have set out to acquire a business facility, we strongly suggest your first move should be to map out your needs in some detail.

Is the Space Efficient?

You can greatly increase the chances that you will acquire a facility making a positive contribution to your bottom line if you carefully consider the functions the facility must perform for efficient operation of your business. We suggest you begin by evaluating the operating steps of your business (that is, the key things you must do in actually providing the goods and services you sell).

Although every small business is different, most small business owners will have to consider a number of issues in selecting a business facility. Not all of the listed items will be important to every small business, and the relative importance of each issue also will vary. Thus, we made no attempt to discuss these items by order of priority. The priority will be for you, the small business owner, to determine, influenced by the general type of business (such as retail or wholesale) and other factors.

Here is a list of common small business requirements that closely relate to the choice of an efficiently functioning business facility:

- **Space for necessary operating steps** — Are the size, construction, condition, age and interior layout suitable for completing the essential steps to bring your product or service to your customers? If not, can modifications be made that are useful and affordable? Consider how many employees you need, and whether they will use specialized machinery. Are there dock and refuse facilities, if needed? Don't forget about functions such as marketing, billing, collection, payroll, facility maintenance and security—all necessary to support the essential steps.

- **Nature of the community** — Is there good traffic flow and ready access to your target buyers? Can you attract and retain qualified employees at an affordable pay rate from the surrounding area? Will suppliers be able to get to you in a timely and cost-efficient manner? Besides these human factors, you should consider the community's character: the costs of local business taxes and zoning regulations, the quality of police and fire departments, rates of insurance coverage, availability of transportation and other services, etc.

- **Nearby businesses and competitors** — In some cases, the absence of competition is considered an advantage. But other times, it's better to be located near a cluster of competitors— the idea being the cluster could attract more customers than any one store could hope to do. Also, you may choose a spot near a large magnet store (one with a large number of customers), so you can piggyback on their high traffic flow.

- **No environmental problems** — Before buying property, have your attorney require the seller or landlord to disclose whether any prior uses had an environmental impact, or any investigations or notices had been done by the federal or state government. Federal law requires clean-up costs to be paid by the owner—whether the owner caused it or not. Protect yourself by doing a thorough investigation before purchasing. Also, if your business uses, generates or receives toxic waste or other environmentally damaging materials, make sure you can obtain and legally use adequate refuse disposal equipment.

- **Satisfactory security** — What are your needs in relation to local crime rates—for your facility, inventory and employees? Does the cost of a security system offset the reduction in rent, or is it a good trade-off? What does it mean for insurance rates?

- **Future growth** — All things being equal, a facility that can accommodate future growth would be more attractive than one that does not. But it usually comes with a cost. So, does it make sense to pay now for the benefit of easy expansion later? Only if you're sure (and not hopeful) of future expansion and if the extra cost won't be a drag on current financial growth.

- **Cost efficiency** — No matter what purposes the facility serves, if it doesn't fit economically into the overall plan for your business, it isn't the ideal facility.

The bottom line: Your facility should do all you want it to. If this is not the case, such as when business operations suffer because the facility is too cramped or inconveniently located, you may need to look for another facility or investigate whether you can operate the business in a way that minimizes the deficiency of the facility.

Example

Joe owns a retail golf-equipment business. He currently keeps his inventory in the back room of his store, which is in a well-located strip mall. However, because he recently expanded his sales floor area to accommodate more equipment displays, his storage area has been reduced to the point where he cannot keep a sufficient inventory.

Ways to deal with Joe's facility problem would include relocating to a larger facility that would accommodate both adequate sales display and inventory space; renting off-site space for storing the overflow inventory; and reducing inventory needs by changing how he does business, such as by utilizing quicker delivery of special-order items from suppliers.

Should You Buy or Lease Your Facility?

New business owners have a tendency to concentrate on the short-term consequences of leasing or buying, such as the first-year cash flow projections that would result for each of the alternatives. This is probably out of necessity: If things don't go well in the first couple of years, your business may not be around to see how a particular decision would have benefited you 10 years down the road.

However, it's a good idea to consider some of the long-term implications. In some cases, buying the facility will be much better for you in the long run, and if you can't afford to buy now, at least you can make it one of your long-term goals.

The main advantage to leasing a facility is that your initial outlay of cash is generally less than it is for purchasing. However, perhaps the main advantage to purchasing is that your facility costs are fixed, and you'll probably end up paying less in the long run than you would have paid if you leased the facility. Moreover, if you purchase, you get the benefit of any appreciation in the value of the property.

When Buying Makes Sense

Aside from the economic issues, the following factors may indicate you should purchase, rather than lease, your business facility:

- **You want control of the property** — Maybe you intend to make substantial additions or renovations to the property. If you own the property, you have much more freedom to make whatever modifications are needed, provided you observe the local zoning laws and building codes.

- **You want to stay at the same location** — For some businesses, such as certain retail and service businesses, location is all-important. If you have established a winning location, you don't want to lose it because of a rent escalation or because the landlord wants the property for another use.

- **You are in an area of appreciating land values** — If you think land values will continue to increase, it would be better to own the property (and thereby get the benefit of this appreciation if you ever sell) rather than to rent it.

When Leasing Makes Sense

The following factors may indicate that you should lease, rather than purchase, your business facility:

- **You don't want maintenance duties** — Many leases place the duty of maintaining the property on the landlord. In that case, you won't have to worry about things like roof repairs, tuck-pointing, maintenance of heating and cooling equipment, plumbing, snow removal and even ordinary housekeeping.

- **You want to retain your mobility** — Maybe you're not sure if your current facility will serve your needs in the future.

- **Your company's credit may not support a mortgage** — If your business is rather new, or has experienced some financial difficulties, lenders may not be willing to extend it sufficient credit for a mortgage on the facility.

- **The facility is in an area of declining real estate values** — You may find a facility that meets your needs, but you also may be concerned about stagnating or dropping real estate values.

Regulatory Matters

Most state and local governments require businesses operating in their area to obtain licenses or permits. In some instances, the federal government may also require you to obtain a license or permit.

There are essentially two types of licenses: general and special. A general license is issued annually for the privilege of operating a business in the jurisdiction. A special license is issued to a business that will provide products or services requiring specific regulation. Special licenses are issued to professionals, such as doctors, lawyers, barbers and others who have met a certain level of training or education, or who engage in an occupation the government considers risky for some reason.

State and local governments regulate the safety, structure and appearance of the community through the use of local laws, called ordinances. Zoning ordinances, which regulate how property can be used, are a common type of ordinance. Once the jurisdiction determines that you have complied with such ordinances, it will issue a permit enabling you to operate your business.

Work Smart

You can find out which licenses and permits are required for your business by calling the state and local government offices in the area in which you are going to operate. Ask them to send you information and any forms that may be required.

If, for some reason, your business is unable or unwilling to comply with an ordinance, you can petition the jurisdiction for a special permit, called a variance, that would allow you, in effect, to violate the ordinance. If you're interested in a variance, call your lawyer. Variances are not routinely granted and can be expensive (in terms of legal fees) to obtain, so make sure you really need it before you request it.

EQUIPPING YOUR NEW BUSINESS

In large part, the type of business you operate will dictate what equipment and other fixed assets you'll require to properly run your business. We can't say exactly what you should acquire without first knowing what you'll be doing. However, we will provide some general points you should consider before you acquire any business equipment, as well as advice on using equipment productively and on disposing of equipment you no longer need.

Save Money

By their nature, fixed assets represent relatively long-term investments of capital. In most cases, it will take several years to recover the money you spend in acquiring the asset, even if everything goes well. Accordingly, unless you have unlimited financial resources, you should avoid acquiring any asset that you can't reasonably expect to bring a significant increase in your profits, efficiency or productivity over the course of the asset's useful life in your business. Be especially careful about tying up capital in fixed assets in response to short-term needs.

So you've concluded your business really does need a particular item of equipment or other fixed asset. Before you rush out and spend some of your valuable capital, invest a little time considering how you can best meet that need. There are basically three alternatives: using assets you already own, purchasing or leasing.

Using Personal Assets

Putting items you already own, such as cars, office furnishings and computer equipment, to work in your business can free up many dollars you would have otherwise spent on acquisition costs. This may seem obvious, but you'd be amazed at how many people spend more money furnishing their office than they could possibly hope to earn in the first year.

If you're conducting business as a sole proprietorship, there's really no trick to converting your personal assets. All it takes is to start using them in your business. For tax purposes, you'll need to know the market value of the item at the time of the conversion—check with your accountant for details. Perhaps your only real concern will be confirming whether you'll lose insurance coverage for the converted items under your homeowner's policy. If so, you'll want to be sure to have the items covered by your business policy.

Saving with Used Equipment

If there's equipment you need but don't already own, be sure to investigate the used equipment market. Depending on the type of item, you may be able to purchase it for a small fraction of what you would have paid if the equipment were new, and without any loss of functionality.

This is especially true for restaurant equipment, store counters and fixtures, office furnishings and, perhaps surprisingly, computers. The equipment is usually generic enough to be adaptable to many different types of businesses, perhaps with some modifications, upgrades or cosmetic improvements.

Where can you find high-quality used equipment? Start by checking the Yellow Pages for listings of thrift stores and secondhand dealers. The classified sections of your local newspaper and trade publications are another good place to look. Be especially watchful for ads mentioning sales related to an office remodeling or business liquidation. And as more people get into—and sometimes out of— home businesses, yard and estate sales also may provide bargains to those with the time and patience to seek them out.

Leasing Your Equipment

Nowadays, you should view leasing companies as potential suppliers for virtually all of your equipment and other tangible business assets. You should have little trouble finding companies willing to lease or rent motor vehicles, office furniture, store fixtures, computers, communications devices, manufacturing equipment and other items you may need. Of course, the trick is determining when you would be better off leasing an asset instead of purchasing it.

By leasing, you can generally gain the use of an asset with less initial cash than you'd need to buy it. Equipment leases rarely require down payments. In other words, leasing may effectively provide the benefit of up to 100-percent financing (although a refundable security deposit may be required in some instances). In contrast, purchase loans frequently require down payments of up to 25 percent or more.

If your startup business is strapped for cash or if you find it difficult to secure the credit necessary to finance your purchases, leasing may be your only real option to obtain needed business assets.

How can you determine whether a lease or a purchase of a given piece of equipment is better for your business? One way is to do a mathematical analysis of your net cash outflows that would result from leasing and from purchasing.

A cash flow analysis provides an estimate of how much cash you would need to set aside today to cover the after-tax costs of each acquisition alternative. The analysis takes into account the "time value of money," which basically is the concept that you don't need to have $50 today to pay a $50 expense at some point in the future, due to the fact you can earn interest on your money.

Case Study — Leasing vs. Purchasing

Let's assume you're faced with the following lease-or-buy decision. You can purchase a $50,000 piece of equipment by putting 25 percent down and paying off the balance at 10 percent interest with four annual installments of $11,830. The equipment will be used in your business for eight years, after which it can be sold for scrap for $2,500. The alternative is that you can lease the same equipment for eight years at an annual rent of $8,500, the first payment of which is due on delivery. You'll be responsible for the equipment's maintenance costs during the lease.

You expect that your combined federal and state income tax rate will be 40 percent for the entire period at issue. You further assume that your cost of capital is 6 percent (the 10-percent financing rate adjusted by your tax rate).

The following tables demonstrate how you can use a cash flow analysis to assist you with a lease-or-buy decision. In this case, if cost were the sole criterion for the decision, you would be inclined to purchase the asset because in current dollars the cost of purchasing is $32,204, while the cost of leasing is $34,838. Even if cost isn't your sole criterion, a cash flow analysis is useful because it can show you how much you're paying for non-cost factors that may dictate your decision to lease.

Cash flow analysis of purchase. *Assume that all payments are made on the first day of the year. Interest is deemed to accrue on the outstanding balance of the loan at the end of each year, and it is computed as follows (the last column shows the portion of each annual payment that goes to principal and that reduces the outstanding loan):*

Breakdown of Loan Payments			
Year End	Outstanding Loan	Interest	Principal
1	37,500	3,750	8,080
2	29,420	2,942	8,888
3	20,532	2,053	9,777
4	10,755	1,075	10,755

Depreciation is computed on the basis of the 200-percent declining balance method.

Breakdown of Cash Flow for Purchasing							
(A) Year	(B) Cash Pmts.	(C) Prior Year's Interest	(D) Prior Year's Dep.	(E) Tax Savings [40% x (C+D)]	(F) Net Cash Flow [B - E]	(G) Discount Factor (6%)	(H) Present Value [F x G]
1	$12,500	$0	$0	$0	$12,500	1.0000	$12,500
2	11,830	0	10,000	4,000	7,830	0.9434	7,387
3	11,830	3,750	16,000	7,900	3,930	0.8900	3,498
4	11,830	2,942	9,600	5,017	6,813	0.8396	5,720
5	11,830	2,053	5,760	3,125	8,705	0.7921	6,895
6		1,075	5,760	2,734	(2,734)	0.7473	(2,043)
7			2,880	1,152	(1,152)	0.7050	(812)
8							
9	(2,500)			(1,000)	(1,500)	0.6274	(941)
Net Cash Flow							$32,204

Cash flow analysis of leasing. Assume that the first lease payment is due on delivery and the following payments are due on the first day of each subsequent year. The business is assumed to have a combined federal and state income tax rate of 40 percent (tax benefits are computed as of the first day of year following the year for which the rental deduction was claimed) and a 6 percent cost of capital.

(A) Year	**(B)** Lease Payment	**(C)** Prior Year's Tax Savings [40% x B]	**(D)** Net Cash Flow [B - C]	**(E)** Discount Factor (6% Cost of Capital)	**(F)** Present Value [D x E]
1	$8,500		$8,500	1.0000	$8,500
2	8,500	3,400	5,100	0.9434	4,811
3	8,500	3,400	5,100	0.8900	4,539
4	8,500	3,400	5,100	0.8396	4,282
5	8,500	3,400	5,100	0.7921	4,040
6	8,500	3,400	5,100	0.7473	3,811
7	8,500	3,400	5,100	0.7050	3,596
8	8,500	3,400	5,100	0.6651	3,392
9		3,400	(3,400)	0.6274	(2,133)
Net Cash Flow					**$34,838**

*Table title: **Breakdown of Cash Flow for Leasing***

Productively Using Your Equipment

There is no right or wrong way to design and equip a workspace. What works for someone else may not work for you. However, we suggest that you keep in mind the following priorities:

- Productive offices are organized so equipment, records management and communications systems not only work, but work together.

- Efficient offices should be both cost-effective and time-effective. If your office is set up right, it allows you to do more, with less money, in less time.

- Comfortable offices help you to do your work with minimal stress and strain on your body.

Disposing of Unproductive Equipment

Every item of equipment you acquire for your business represents an investment of your business capital. Taken a step further, an item not currently being used represents capital on which the current return is zero or even negative (if property taxes and insurance costs attributable to the item are taken into account).

Adopt a practice of taking regular inventories of all your equipment to confirm each item's current level of use. If you come across an item you're currently not using, try to determine whether you have a definite future use for the item that justifies the continuing cost of holding it. Otherwise, consider selling or disposing of the item.

If you're unable to sell an unproductive item of equipment, or to use it as a trade-in on the purchase of an item you need, you may be able to generate a tax deduction by donating the item to charity or by simply abandoning (junking) it.

Chapter 9

Recruiting and Hiring

You've chosen a site and you're in the process of equipping it to conduct business. Depending on the scope of your operation, the next requirement before opening the doors to your new ideal facility may be recruiting and hiring employees.

Maybe your business plan always called for employees to help run operations. Or maybe during the setup phase you find the work is getting to be too much, so you're thinking about adding staff to help out. Either way, before you hire help, you must ask yourself if you really need to hire someone or just be better organized. If you're having trouble getting organized, try libraries, community centers or colleges for time-management courses.

In this chapter, we'll consider the various classes of employees in an effort to define the type of work you need done. With that in mind, we'll examine how to establish job qualifications and descriptions, so you can find and hire the right people. And we'll also show you how to protect yourself from potential litigation arising from the hiring process. There's a lot of government regulation in this area that you need to be aware of.

Finally, we'll go through the numerous considerations inherent in setting up a payroll system to compensate your employees . . . and the federal and state governments. This can get rather complicated, so you'll need to understand how to follow the rules.

TYPES OF HELP AVAILABLE

If you believe you need someone to help take over part of your workload, there are a number of staffing options to choose from:

- **Full-time employees** — Because most people work only one full-time job, you are more likely to have control over the employee's time and to get increased employee loyalty. Also, you may have the peace of mind there will be someone around to mind the store in your absence. On the other hand, full-time employees are covered by numerous labor laws and may expect benefits such as health insurance and paid vacations. Will you have to provide these types of benefits to be competitive?

- **Part-time employees** — This option allows you to have control over the employees' work, generally at a lower cost, but at the sacrifice of employee loyalty. As a rule, part-timers don't get as many benefits as full-time employees and are often willing to adjust their schedules according to the amount of work available. Of course, they also could leave your business if an offer of full-time employment comes along, so you may end up with an employee turnover problem.

- **Temporary help** — Traditionally, temporary help firms have been useful in replacing full-time employees for the short term. But by using temps for longer-term vacancies, you may save on payroll administration and fringe benefits, since you'll only have to cut one check to the agency each period. The agency also will do the recruiting and send you qualified people, thus saving you time. But you will pay more for this convenience. And with no long-term commitment from the temp, you may tire of training a series of workers who leave at unpredictable times. On the upside, you may be able to convince a good temp to work for you permanently, avoiding the risks of a probationary period.

- **Leased employees** — This generally refers to a situation where another business "employs" your staff—which includes doing the payroll, administering benefits, etc.—and you pay them a fee plus expenses to do it. Ultimately, this might be cheaper than doing it yourself. In many cases, the leasing agency simply takes over your existing staff of permanent employees with little change in the actual makeup of your work force. Because leasing companies aggregate the employees of many companies in negotiating for health insurance, pensions, etc., you can sometimes provide more benefits at a much lower cost.

Work Smart

If you're going to use an employee leasing firm, be careful in how you communicate the new arrangement to your existing employees. They may find it unsettling if they don't understand the leasing arrangement is mainly on paper, and they aren't really losing their jobs. One way to overcome this fear is to have your employees meet with current employees of the leasing company who have successfully made the transition.

- **Independent contractors** — Under this classification, it's possible to have personnel working on (or off) your premises without becoming subject to payroll taxes, or to many state and federal employment laws. Independent contractors usually are signed to a contract for a special skilled project expected to last a relatively short length of time. In most cases, you establish the project outline and due date, and they determine how to accomplish it, on their own schedule. They are generally paid based on results (i.e., a flat rate per job, or a per-unit-completed rate) rather than by the hour. For tax purposes, a worker will be treated as an employee if the business owner has the right to determine not just what the employee does, but when, where or how the worker does it. Traditionally, the IRS has closely scrutinized the use of independent contractors, and in borderline situations it is likely to rule the workers are really employees. Consult your attorney regarding the complex details of using this type of help.

Exempt vs. Nonexempt Status

The federal Fair Labor Standards Act (FLSA) sets forth additional guidelines for the classification of employees by type. Foremost among those laws is the notion of exempt and nonexempt workers. Your responsibilities under the FLSA will vary tremendously depending on how each employee is classified under the law. Exempt employees aren't entitled to the benefits and protections of the FLSA, including minimum wage and overtime rules; nonexempt employees are protected by the FLSA.

Did You Know?

Employees who are paid at an hourly rate, instead of a salary, are nonexempt. This means the employees are protected by the federal Fair Labor Standards Act. Employees who are paid a salary may or may not be exempt, depending on the type of work they do. Executives, administrative staff, managers and professionals (doctors, lawyers, teachers, artists, etc.) are usually exempt.

Employees with nonexempt status are entitled to the following protections under the FLSA:

- **Minimum wage** — For each hour worked up to 40 hours in a calendar workweek, a minimum pay rate of $5.15 per hour must be used. For employees who receive tips, the minimum pay rate is $2.13 per hour, provided the weekly average of hourly tip money makes up the balance ($3.02). Otherwise, the employer must make up the difference. Some states statutes provide different regulations for minimum wage and tip credit; the rule is that you must pay the higher of the federal or state minimum that applies to you. Check with the appropriate state employment authorities to see what the law requires in your state.

- **Overtime pay** — For each hour worked in excess of 40 hours in a calendar workweek, a pay rate of $1^1/_2$ times the regular hourly rate must be used ($7.73 for minimum wage earners). Some states also have regulations regarding overtime pay, and whichever law (federal or state) is more generous to the employee is the one that applies. Check with the proper state employment authorities to learn about your particular obligations.

Employees with exempt status include executives who spend at least half their time exercising managerial functions; administrative staff; and professionals, such as attorneys, doctors, artists or teachers. Other employees who aren't protected by all parts of the FLSA include learners, apprentices and full-time students employed in agriculture or retailing; outside sales staff; employees at amusement or recreational establishments with seasonal peaks; certain workers with disabilities; and employees who deliver newspapers to consumers. Even if you and your employees aren't subject to the guidelines of the FLSA (which is unlikely), always keep the exempt/nonexempt distinction in mind when recruiting and hiring.

DEFINING THE JOB YOU NEED DONE

Once the decision is made to hire someone, you must determine exactly what you want the person to do for your business. Particularly if you are hiring that first employee, try to narrow it down into a list of specific tasks before you decide what job qualifications you'll be looking for. Later on, you can use your list to write your job description and, ultimately, train your new employee.

One approach is to consider which of your current duties could be taught easily to a new employee. Another approach is to think about the skills you and your other employees are lacking, then try to fill those needs.

Establishing Job Qualifications

After you've done some investigation into what the job should entail, the skills and areas of knowledge required should be translated into your job qualifications. Qualifications include such things as experience, education, ability, language skills, and physical strength or agility. You'll want to keep these qualifications in mind as you review applications and interview people for the job.

If you need an administrative assistant who can type, answer phones and file, chances are you'll need someone with good organizational skills. Instead of requiring one year of clerical duties, you might find a person who does not have clerical experience, per se, but who was, for example, an assistant manager at a department store or a server in a restaurant. This person might have some of the same sets of skills and abilities.

Remember, federal and state laws place restrictions on using job qualifications that could result in discrimination against people on the basis of race, color, religion, sex, national origin, citizenship, disability or age (see page 160). Here are some of the legal ramifications you should keep in mind when defining the position you need filled:

- **Ability and experience** — Judging a candidate's ability can be difficult. Sometimes it is an innate, personal trait, and other times it is a by-product of education or experience. In many cases, you'll have to judge the candidate's ability by asking for information about past job experiences or by administering an achievement test. In most cases, the ideal candidate will have at least some exposure and experience in the necessary job skills. The important thing, from a legal standpoint, is not to define your experience baseline so strictly that you disqualify people who could do the job.

- **Education** — Most employers require at least a high school degree or an equivalency certificate for most jobs. Some positions require more advanced thought and responsibilities, and therefore may require more advanced education. For employers of 15 or more, the Equal Employment Opportunity Commission only requires that educational requirements can't be set so high they tend to restrict certain protected groups of people from getting hired or promoted. If you do require a degree or level of educational attainment, be prepared to justify why the degree itself is a necessary requirement, as opposed to the ability to do certain types of work.

- **English language fluency** — As with all skills and abilities, to avoid problems with civil rights laws, language fluency must be related to the performance of the job in order to be required. This doesn't mean it is *desirable* to have proficiency in the language; it must be an *important* part of the job. For instance, refusing to hire computer programmers with "poor grammar" was found to be unlawful bias by one court, since grammar skills were not an important part of the job.

- **Physical effort or strength** — Some jobs may require certain physical abilities or strengths. To avoid problems with workers' compensation and safety, these requirements should definitely be a part of your written job description. If you employ 15 or more people, and are therefore subject to the Americans with Disabilities Act (ADA), the basic tenets of the law require that, if an employee can do the *essential functions* of a job with *reasonable accommodation*, then the employee should not be discriminated against in the hiring process. Reasonable accommodation is a rather technical concept. If you suspect you may face this issue during the hiring process, check with your lawyer.

Creating Job Descriptions

If you're just hiring one person, perhaps your first employee, you don't need to write a formal job description unless you want to. Job descriptions aren't required by law for *any* employer, but they're good to have for several reasons. A job description can help when you're interviewing, explaining a job to a new employee or evaluating an employee's performance. It also provides evidence of your fair hiring practices, should you ever have to defend them in court.

You've already analyzed, to the extent you can, what the position entails. You've also identified the skills and qualifications needed to do the job effectively. A job description blends these two elements into a single document that is a blueprint for the job and a logical precursor to writing a job ad. Here's how to proceed.

- Jot down a few key words for each task that might go into a job description (e.g., "greeting customers").

- Rank the tasks in terms of importance (and frequency or time commitment, if those factors are relevant).

- List the activities involved in doing each task. For example, to "greet customers," an employee might handle the telephones, welcome customers to the office and answer questions.

- List the skills and abilities necessary to perform that activity. Continuing the previous example, skills might be "pleasant phone voice," "strong speaking skills," "good organizational skills," "tremendous patience" and "a working knowledge of the business."

HIRING EMPLOYEES

As soon as you've formulated a job description, and researched an appropriate salary and benefits package for your situation, you'll need to publicize your job opening. There are many avenues for seeking employment help: run an electronic or print ad in newspapers, trade journals, or on television or radio; recruit at job fairs or schools; or use public or private employment agencies. One or more of these methods should work for you.

Then, once you've spread the word, it's time to deal with the people who apply for your job opening, and there's no way to predict how many will respond. This is particularly true if you're hiring for the first time. So be prepared to deal with the disappointment of receiving few or no applications, or the panic of trying to deal with hundreds of responses.

Screening Applicants

While looking for prospective employees, it's important to recognize you'll be diverting some time and attention from your regular business activities. Applicants will want to meet with you before or after regular working hours, during your regular working hours, or at lunch. Do your best to accommodate qualified applicants, but don't let the hiring process have a negative impact on your business.

Hiring also means you'll also be spending time verifying information provided in resumes or job applications. This may include background checks, employment and personal reference checks, and even credit checks. You may even want to give a test to your applicants, if testing will provide information you need to find the best person for the job. The steps you take will vary based on the nature of the job you're trying to fill.

Example

If you're hiring someone to make deliveries, an applicant's driving record is extremely significant. You'd be less interested in the driving record of a person applying to be a cashier, who won't ever drive a company vehicle. In contrast, you'd be a lot more interested in checking references and background information relating to that person's honesty and ability to deal with numerous cash transactions.

Making Your Selection

After you've selected the person you want to hire, you'll have to make an offer and work out the terms of the person's employment. Prospective employees have become increasingly likely to want to negotiate starting pay, vacations and other issues. In many cases, you may have to make some concessions to get the person you want. Only agree to an arrangement if you're comfortable with it. If you think a prospective employee is being unreasonable, don't offer the job. After all, you're likely to have a long-term relationship with the new hire, and you don't want to start out on the wrong foot.

Once an applicant accepts your offer, you still have some work to do to get ready for the employee's first day. You'll need to prepare some kind of orientation for the new employee to introduce him or her to how you do business and what your expectations are. Don't make the mistake of merely showing your new employee where to sit and assuming that the rest will be picked up by osmosis. Like it or not, for at least a little while, it's in your best interest to be a teacher as well as a business owner and an employer.

You'll also be required by law to create certain records and fill out government paperwork. Among the items you must file:

- **Form W-4** — The Form W-4 must be completed by every employee so you know how much federal income tax to withhold from your new employee's wages. The importance of filing a Withholding Allowance Certificate, Form W-4, cannot be overstated, so make its completion a priority.

- **Form I-9** — Under the Immigration Reform and Control Act of 1986, all employers are required to verify the identity and the eligibility to work in the United States of all employees hired after November 6, 1986, using the Bureau of Citizenship and Immigration Services (BCIS) Form I-9, *Employment Eligibility Verification Form*. Once completed, the form isn't sent to the government, but you must keep it in your files in case a BCIS inspector ever wants to see it. The I-9 form lists acceptable forms of documentation for proving identity and eligibility to work.

Work Smart

Form W-4 is currently available from the IRS web site at http://www.irs.ustreas.gov/prod/cover.html. In addition, Form I-9 is available from the Bureau of Citizenship and Immigration Services web site at http://www.immigration.gov/graphics/formsfree/forms/index.html.

- **New hire reporting required by state law** — Federal law requires all employers, even those with just one employee, to report all new hires to the appropriate state agency. In turn, these state agencies must turn over the information to a national directory of new hires, maintained by the Department of Health and Human Services. The information will be used primarily for two purposes. First, it will help prevent unemployment compensation fraud. Second, it will make it possible to track down parents who owe child support.

Did You Know?

In conjunction with the new hire reporting requirements, all states are also required to establish and maintain databases of every child support order entered in the state. Each state is required to match the new hire information against those child support orders. The federal government has a similar, nationwide database and uses it to catch deadbeat parents who have moved to another state. You may be obligated to withhold from an employee's wages if he or she is making support payments.

- **Employee records** — There is no law that requires you to keep a personnel file on each employee. *Specific employee information* is what you must retain for at least three years under federal laws. However, as a practical matter, personnel files are the easiest means of keeping track of employee information and complying with these requirements. Information collected about employees and retained in personnel files should be strictly job-related. For bare-bones compliance, include full name and employee number (or Social Security number); home address, including zip code; date of birth; gender; job title; basic payroll records; and the I-9 form.

Work Smart

Although the law requires larger employers to keep information relating to employment actions for a year, how long you choose to keep them after that is up to you. There are two schools of thought regarding how long to keep records.

On the one hand, it makes sense to establish a policy of clearing out outdated records on a periodic basis. It saves space and time. Further, if an employee or applicant subsequently challenges the basis for an employment action you took, and you've discarded the records, it will be difficult to establish that your decision was improper in the absence of any written records of how the decision was reached. Those taking this approach work under the assumption that a creative lawyer might be able to find some proof of discrimination in almost anyone's records.

On the other hand, some people feel retaining this type of information may work in their favor. If someone charges you with hiring discrimination, for example, your records can establish your hiring process has always been fair and nondiscriminatory. If you agree, we suggest you keep personnel records for seven years after an employee leaves.

In addition to the basic information you're required to keep for three years, you also have to keep records relating to your hiring procedures and to job applicants you didn't hire. In general, federal law requires you to keep these records for at least one year if you have 15 employees or more. If you do, the documents you must keep include:

- completed job applications, resumes, and other forms of employment inquiries and hiring materials

- job orders submitted to employment agencies and any ads related to job openings

- records of promotions, demotions, transfers and other job actions

- copies of any tests or examinations administered and the results of those tests (including physical testing)

- materials relating to selection for training or apprenticeship

- employee requests for physical job accommodation

- materials relating to layoffs or termination

Avoiding Negligent Hiring

You can be legally liable for negligent hiring if you fail to check references, criminal records or background and, as a result, hire someone who harms another employee, a customer or some other business contact. Someone can sue, and possibly recover damages from you, for your failure to take reasonable steps to discover an employee's unfitness for a position or your subsequent failure to take corrective action, such as training, reassignment or discharge.

If you're served with a negligent hiring lawsuit, immediately call your lawyer. He or she can tell you more about your chances for winning or losing the lawsuit. Basically, however, you're at serious risk if your employee was at least partly to blame for the incident.

Example

A furniture store owner was liable for negligent hiring when a delivery person assaulted a customer while delivering furniture to her home. A routine background check would have revealed that he had a history of violent behavior. The customer could recover damages from the owner in this instance because it was reasonably foreseeable that a person with a violent past might attack a customer.

A closely related concept is negligent *retention*. In this situation, someone will attempt to hold you liable for the conduct of an employee you should have terminated. If you become aware that an employee is unfit, but let the employee continue to work, you're opening up yourself to charges of negligent retention. Your best defense is to take immediate corrective or remedial action upon discovering a problem employee.

Some states have laws requiring criminal background checks on workers in certain occupations, such as child care or senior care workers. For more information, check the *CCH Business Owner's Toolkit* web site at http://www.toolkit.cch.com.

Setting Basic Workplace Rules

If you hire employees, you'll need to think about establishing some basic ground rules. It's important to make sure your employees understand what is expected of them, not only in the work they do, but in their behavior and in other areas of the employment relationship. While some think of these rules as nothing more than a necessary evil, if they are carefully selected, clearly related to business and fairly enforced, they can help you to better manage your workplace and your workers.

The federal and state governments have mandated some policies that affect the employer/employee relationship. These laws may require you to establish certain rules to ensure compliance with these policies (see page 160).

Some optional types of work rules are valuable as well. They help create and maintain an orderly atmosphere where it is pleasant to work and easier to work effectively. This is to your benefit because employees tend to be more creative and productive when they are content. Some rules also improve quality of work life by ensuring professional and safe conduct, encouraging open lines of communication, and guaranteeing fair and equitable treatment of all. On the other hand, if your rules are unreasonable, inappropriate or unenforced, employee morale may be damaged.

It's best to keep the rules as general as possible, so you have as much flexibility as possible in enforcing them. Consider using a simple one- or two-page handout with an opening statement like: "It would be impractical to set forth a list of all activities considered to be illegal or contrary to good business practices and good employee-employer relations. This is intended only as a guideline."

Then, draft a set of rules on these subjects: safety, absence and tardiness, working hours and overtime, break and lunch periods, telephone usage, alcohol/illicit drug abuse, dress code, use of or damage to company property, and confidentiality of sensitive information.

Finally, you may also want to explain the consequences and discipline an employee may expect for breaking the rules. But again, build some flexibility into your system by including a general statement that "any employee found engaging in these behaviors may be subject to disciplinary actions including reprimand, warning, layoff or dismissal."

EMPLOYERS' LEGAL RESPONSIBILITIES

If you decide to hire help, it's extremely important to be aware of the numerous federal and state laws possibly affecting the employment relationship. These laws cover topics as diverse as minimum wages, discrimination, required leave and smoking, and they are intended to prevent the unfair treatment of people in identified segments of the population. Whether or not your business is subject to specific employment laws depends on how many employees you have and how long they've worked for you. In some states, you're subject to certain laws if you have even one employee.

Did You Know?

Protected groups are groups of people that are distinguished by special characteristics such as their race, color, ethnicity, national origin, religion, gender, age (over 40), disability or veteran status. Generally speaking, people in these groups can't be discriminated against in any facet of employment, including hiring, promotion, training, discipline, pay and termination. Some states afford protection to other groups, such as people in different age groups, those who smoke, and individuals with a particular sexual orientation.

Take your responsibility to comply with laws against employment discrimination very seriously. If you do not and later are sued, you open up yourself to the possibility of huge damage awards if you are unable to prove you didn't violate these laws.

Anti-discrimination laws aren't unreasonable or inflexible; they recognize some situations in which it's necessary to exclude certain people from consideration for employment. Foremost among these exceptions is the concept of bona fide occupational qualifications.

Example

Some federal and state employment laws permit employers to make employment decisions based on otherwise prohibited factors when it is "reasonably necessary to the normal operation of that particular business or enterprise." For example, a religious school may require its teachers to be practicing members of the religion being taught because it is a bona fide occupational qualification.

Your Federal Obligations

The following table provides an overview of the major federal fair employment laws. Normally, these laws become applicable at the start of the hiring process and continue through the termination of the employment relationship.

Federal Employment Laws

Federal Law	*What It Does*	*Who Has To Comply*
Fair Labor Standards Act (FLSA)	Requires you to pay minimum wage and overtime pay to nonexempt workers.	All employers of employees engaged in interstate commerce[1].
Occupational Safety and Health Act (OSHA)	Requires you to maintain a safe workplace and comply with specific safety standards and recordkeeping rules.	All employers, but in states where a federally certified plan has been adopted, the state plan governs.
Federal Insurance Contributions Act (FICA)	Requires you to pay Social Security and Medicare taxes, and withhold such taxes from workers' pay.	All employers.
Federal Unemployment Tax Act (FUTA)	Requires you to pay federal unemployment payroll taxes.	All employers.
Equal Pay Act	Requires equal pay for men and women who perform the same work.	All employers.
National Labor Relations Act	Prohibits discrimination against employees who engage in or refuse to engage in union activity. Protects nonunion employees who act together in an effort to improve or protest working conditions.	Employers whose business has a significant impact on interstate commerce.
Employee Retirement Income Security Act (ERISA)	Prohibits employees from being discharged solely to prevent vesting or qualifying for benefits under qualified pension plans.	Employers who maintain qualified pension plans for their employees' benefit.
Immigration Reform and Control Act	Prohibits discrimination against employees on the basis of national origin or citizenship.	Employers having at least four employees.
Americans With Disabilities Act (ADA)	Prohibits discrimination against disabled employees.	Employers having at least 15 employees.
Civil Rights Act, Title VII	Prohibits discrimination against employees on the basis of race, color, religion, sex or national origin.	Employers having at least 15 employees.
Age Discrimination in Employment Act (ADEA)	Prohibits age-based discrimination against employees who are 40 years or older.	Employers having at least 20 employees.
Family and Medical Leave Act (FMLA)	Requires employers to grant up to 12 weeks' unpaid leave per year for certain medical conditions of a worker or family member, or for new births or adoptions.	Employers having at least 50 employees.

[1]Note that courts routinely find that virtually all businesses have an impact on interstate commerce. Shipping goods to, or acquiring materials from, another state is frequently sufficient to satisfy this requirement.

Your State Obligations

Other than state tax laws, state employment discrimination laws are considered to have the biggest potential impact on small businesses. Only employers who have 15 or more employees are subject to the most complex and comprehensive federal anti-discrimination laws (20 or more employees in the case of age discrimination). However, in some states, employers with just one employee are subject to state anti-discrimination laws. You can be exempt from federal laws, yet still be subject to your state's civil rights laws. And some state laws are broader in scope and coverage than similar federal laws.

Every state has enacted various laws pertaining to employment discrimination, in regard to any or all of the following: sex, race, creed, color, national origin, age, disability, marital status, religion, sexual orientation, illness or other classifications. Many states have both fair labor laws of general application plus targeted laws that address single issues, such as age discrimination. In general, these laws prohibit employers from refusing employment; discharging an employee; or discriminating in compensation or the terms, conditions or privileges of employment.

Warning

Almost every state bars employers from retaliating against employees who oppose or report improper employment practices (whistleblowers). They also prohibit employers from discriminating against employees whose wages are garnished for child support, alimony or other debts.

Many states exempt the employment of immediate family members from their employment discrimination rules. In addition, although most states prohibit discrimination based on disability, an employer may take employment actions based on disability where it is not possible to reasonably accommodate the disabled employee.

Another important obligation is compliance with workers' compensation laws that protect employees against loss of income and pay medical bills resulting from a work-related injury, accident, illness or disease. In the vast majority of states, this insurance coverage is mandatory.

Workers' compensation insurance limits your liability for on-the-job injuries to the remedies available under the system; you can't be sued for everything you own. It provides wage-loss, medical and death benefits to workers regardless of who caused the injury, although employees retain the right to sue third parties for their negligence. Wages are usually covered at a rate of one-half to two-thirds regular pay.

To purchase coverage, you can choose from your state's menu of options, which generally include a state insurance pool, individual insurance with private companies or self-insurance by the employer. The state pool is usually the least expensive choice.

Each state's laws regarding all these obligations are different. Most states determine who is subject to the law based on the minimum number of employees in an enterprise (the threshold), and your state's laws may not apply to you, depending on the size of your business and, occasionally, other factors as well. For more information, check out our web site at http://www.toolkit.cch.com. We suggest you consult an attorney and take whatever steps are necessary to comply with all applicable rules.

PAYROLL CONSIDERATIONS

If you choose to hire employees, you'll have to set up a payroll system to compensate them. And doing the payroll obviously is much more complicated than just writing out a check to each employee every week or two. Numerous federal and state laws come into play, dictating how you must calculate the employees' pay and any overtime required, make any necessary deductions from paychecks, and get the pay into the workers' hands.

A large part of correctly doing payroll is being aware of and complying with payroll tax laws. Not only must you calculate the taxes, you must deduct some tax from employees' paychecks, pay some yourself and deposit them with the government's bankers within tight deadlines.

This is where your accountant could really be helpful. But if you decide to go it alone, at least use an accounting software package that includes a payroll module. It'll make your life a lot easier.

Payroll System Requirements

Here are the steps in setting up a successful payroll program:

- **Federal Employer Identification Number** — Every employer must file for an EIN from the IRS by using Form SS-4.

- **State/local identification numbers** — You may also need to get identification or account numbers from the various state and local taxing jurisdictions to which you will be reporting, depositing and paying taxes. In many states, the federal EIN also is used for state income tax reporting purposes. Call your state department of revenue to find out how to get a number.

- **Classify your employees** — You must determine whether

your workers are independent contractors or employees who will require payroll tax deductions.

- **Social Security numbers** — You will need these numbers from all workers, even independent contractors.

- **W-4 forms** — You will also need a signed form from all employees. Do this upon hiring. The form contains pertinent employee information, including claiming allowances for federal and state income tax withholding.   .

- **Establish a pay period** — The length of the payroll period is important, mainly because it determines the method for withholding federal income tax. It also triggers the date and timing of payments you owe the government for payroll taxes. While no federal laws require you to pay employees at regular intervals, most state laws mandate that every employer must pay all wages due to its employees on regular paydays designated in advance by the employer—usually twice a month, although some states statutes only require payment once a month.

Once you've done these things, you can begin paying employees by figuring the hours they've worked, determining what their regular rate of pay is, taking tax and other deductions from their checks, and getting the money to employees.

Paying Payroll Taxes

Once you assume the role of an employer, you will be required to withhold taxes from your employees' pay and to deposit the withheld amounts with the appropriate tax agencies. Furthermore, as an employer, you'll be personally liable for paying certain taxes on the amounts you pay your workers.

Together, those taxes that you're required to withhold and those that you're directly required to pay comprise your payroll taxes. Specifically, by hiring employees, you take on the following payroll tax obligations:

- **Withhold federal, state and local income taxes** — Although the law provides specific rules for calculating the amount owed, the IRS and your state tax agencies have reduced the rules to simple tax tables that you can use in most cases. You can get the federal tax tables by calling 1-800-TAX-FORM and asking for Circular E and its supplement. Contact your state and local governments for information on their tax laws.

- **Withhold and pay Social Security and Medicare taxes** — The Federal Insurance Contributions Act (FICA) requires you to withhold a Social Security tax and a Medicare tax from the wages you pay. In 2003, for example, the Social Security tax rate on employees is 6.2 percent on the first $87,000 you pay each employee, and the Medicare tax rate is 1.45 percent on all wages whatever the amount. To compute the tax withheld, you merely multiply an employee's gross wage payment, including certain fringe benefits, by the applicable tax rate. Then, the law also requires you as the employer to pay an equal amount of these taxes on each employee's behalf.

- **Pay federal and state unemployment taxes** — The unemployment benefit system is a combined federal-state program, and as an employer, if you meet the minimum criteria, you'll generally have to pay both federal and state unemployment taxes. The federal tax rate is a flat 6.2 percent for the first $7,000 of each employee's wages, but you can claim a credit against this tax of 5.4 percent if you paid your state unemployment taxes on time. As a result, your actual effective rate for federal tax is 0.8 percent. Contact your state unemployment agency regarding your state tax obligations, which vary from state to state.

- **Pay and/or withhold state disability insurance taxes** — California, Hawaii, New Jersey, New York, Puerto Rico and Rhode Island require you to pay short-term disability insurance tax. All six places, *except* Rhode Island, allow an employer to opt out of the state plan and to put the employee contributions into a private plan. The plans must meet state requirements regarding coverage, eligibility, contribution amounts, and employee approval. Contact your state employment agency regarding these rules.

- **Pay on time and file required returns or reports** — For federal payroll taxes, this usually means depositing the taxes with an authorized financial institution on at least a monthly basis, and filing quarterly or annual returns. For most state payroll taxes, you usually send your payment with an accompanying return on a quarterly basis, directly to the agency that administers the particular tax.

However, your payroll obligations do not end there. You also have reporting requirements (in the form of W-2s) to your employees and, in some cases, independent contractors. Furthermore, you must maintain all records pertaining to payroll taxes and wages paid.

Paying Yourself

Even if you don't hire anyone else to help you run your business, you're always going to have at least one employee—you. So, what kind of payroll tax obligations do you have with respect to yourself?

If you organize your business as a corporation, you're likely to have all the same obligations you would have if you actually hired another employee. This is because corporations are treated as distinct legal entities from their founders and shareholders. If you do work for the corporation, you'll generally be treated as its employee, even if you are the sole shareholder.

But what if you don't incorporate? For starters, although you won't have to go through the formalities of withholding income taxes and payroll taxes from the income you draw from your business, you may have to make regular estimated tax payments, based on your quarterly net profits from the business.

Moreover, if you earn at least $400 a year from your business, you'll have to pay self-employment taxes. In essence, self-employment taxes are FICA taxes imposed on those who are in business for themselves.

Like the FICA taxes, the self-employment taxes consist of a Social Security tax and a Medicare tax. In 2003, for example, the total rate is 15.3 percent, with a Social Security rate of 12.4 percent on the first $87,000 you earn and a Medicare rate of 2.9 percent on all your earnings—the same rates you would get by adding the employer and employee portions of the FICA taxes together. The self-employment taxes are imposed on your net self-employment income, which is basically your business income reduced by your business deductions. You report the tax on your annual income tax return, and you must include it in the amount you owe for estimated income tax payment purposes.

Chapter 10

Figuring the Cost
Of Opening Your Doors

The dream is nearly a reality. Most of the initial decisions have been made: You know what kind of business to launch, where it will be, how it will be organized, who it will serve, and why it should be successful. But how much will it actually cost?

Earlier in Chapter 3, we analyzed the startup expenses for your new business. Back then, only a ballpark estimate was required, because you were trying to see if you could personally afford to go into business.

But now, since you are much closer to actually going into business for yourself, you'll need to go into a little more detail regarding startup expenses. As we've said before, one of the main reasons that new businesses fail is too little money. To avoid this, you need to account for all of your expenses, from the moment you start investigating your business idea to the time you open doors and beyond.

Actually, you should have been refining your ballpark estimate as you went along. Over time, the individual costs of various items in the startup process become more apparent. And as the big picture comes more into focus, so should your business's overall financial needs.

At this point, it's time to take an overview of all the little (and not so little) costs. For our purposes, expenses should be broken down into two categories: startup and the first 90 days. Remember, you should expect cash flow to be pretty slow during these periods, so you'll want to be ready for it by anticipating costs as best you can.

But to do this properly, you'll need to have a system in place to keep track of these costs as you incur them. And you must have a complete understanding of how best to use your recordkeeping system to your advantage.

FINANCIAL RECORDKEEPING

By now, you've established a series of plans and strategies for achieving financial success with your new business. But inherent in executing these objectives is the notion of good financial recordkeeping. Not only must you plan for success, you must monitor and record your efforts. And you must know how to make the process work for you.

For example, in an effort to encourage people to open up new small businesses, Congress has used the Internal Revenue Code to provide certain financial benefits to small business owners. Of particular interest is the provision allowing the deduction, over a 60-month period, of expenses incurred to start the business.

This is an important exception to the general rule that expenses are deductible only if they relate to an existing business. In addition, the costs of *investigating a business opportunity* are included in the startup expenses that may be amortized, provided the investigative activities actually lead to an operating business.

Warning

The 60-month amortization of startup costs applies only to the costs incurred investigating a new business and to those expenses that would be deductible by an existing business. Organizational expenses, such as the costs you incur to incorporate or to form a partnership, don't qualify as startup expenses, but can be separately amortized over the 60 months following the formation of the partnership or corporation. Real estate taxes and mortgage interest that are deductible under other law provisions are excluded from the amortized startup expenses.

This provision alone should be enough to convince you to get a financial recordkeeping system in place as soon as you decide to start your business. You have an immediate need to track the expenses to start the business so you can deduct them after your business is up and running. Moreover, it also will help you in the long run because you'll become proficient at bookkeeping (or, at least, at dealing with a bookkeeper) before you take on accounting for a going concern.

Eventually, you'll need to have a bookkeeping system in place at the time you first open your doors. For now, you'll primarily track expenses in the pre-opening phase of your business, but your system must also allow for the accurate reflection of income as it is received. Thus, there are both short-term and long-term benefits to deciding to set up an accounting system now. As we'll discuss shortly, this decision will be vitally important when you do need the services of an accountant.

Importance of Good Records

While we're citing the immediate need to track pre-opening expenses to convince you to start keeping records right now, there are other reasons why it's important to keep accurate financial records. As a business owner, you'll perform a wide variety of activities absolutely requiring you to have books that clearly reflect the results of your business operations. Here's just a few of them.

- **Monitoring success or failure** — It's hard to know how your business is doing without a clear financial picture. Am I making money? Are sales increasing? Are expenditures increasing faster than sales? Which expenses are too high based on my level of sales? Do some expenditures appear to be out of control?

- **Providing needed information** — Evaluating the financial consequences should be a factor in every business decision you make. Without accurate records and financial information, it may be hard for you to know the financial impact of a given course of action. Will it pay to hire another salesperson? How much will another production employee cost? Is this particular product line profitable?

- **Obtaining bank financing** — Besides the usual financial statements—a balance sheet, income statement, and cash flow budget for the most current and prior years, as well as your projected statements showing the impact of the requested loan—a banker may even want to see some of your bookkeeping procedures and documents to verify whether you run your business in a sound, professional manner.

- **Obtaining capital from other sources** — If you are thinking of taking on a partner or an outside investor, you'll need to produce a lot of financial information. Even your suppliers and other creditors may ask to see certain financial records. Such information may be produced by your outside accountant, but it's based on your day-to-day recordkeeping.

- **Budgeting** — All businesses should use a meaningful budget for planning purposes, such as forecasting cash needs and helping control expenditures. In addition, if you are seeking bank financing or other sources of capital, a banker or prospective investor will probably want to see your budget as evidence your business is well planned and stable.

- **Preparing income taxes** — With good records, completing this process will be easier, more accurate and, most likely, on time. Poor records may result in underpaying or overpaying your taxes and/or filing late (and paying penalties). If your accountant prepares your income tax return, poor records will almost certainly result in higher accounting fees.

- **Complying with federal and state payroll taxes** — If you hire employees, there are myriad rules and regulations relating to payroll taxes. Payroll tax deposits must be made according to strict deadlines. Late payment of payroll taxes results in severe, and unnecessary, penalties. Also, you must file a payroll tax return every quarter, which you must reconcile with the payroll deposits made during the quarter. Then at the end of the year, you are required to give your employees and the government W-2 forms, which must agree with your quarterly payroll returns.

- **Submitting sales taxes** — If you collect sales tax from your customers, good records will make it easy for you to compute the tax due and prepare the required reports.

- **Distributing profits** — If your business is a partnership, you will need good records to determine the correct amount of profits to distribute to each partner. If you are operating as a corporation, you must determine the company profits that will be paid out as dividends to the shareholders.

Accounting and Bookkeeping Basics

Because you're in the process of starting a business, the focus here is on these accounting and bookkeeping activities that relate to the pre-opening expenses you'll incur. Presumably, you won't be receiving any income at this point; that won't begin until you actually open up for business. Nevertheless, we'll look at the entire accounting system you'll have to have in place when you begin doing business.

In Chapter 4, we discussed the process used to select an accountant to work with as you build your business. Many small business owners rely on an outside accountant to do their taxes and prepare financial statements. However, you'll likely find it's too expensive to pay an accountant to do routine bookkeeping chores. You (or someone in your organization) will have to take on the responsibility of keeping an accurate set of financial records. Fortunately, you may find this task easier than you thought, especially if you use your computer.

Accounting Terms

The goal of an accounting system is to provide current, accurate information regarding the source and use of funds by your business.

Don't underestimate the importance of a good accounting system. Remember, a large number of businesses fail each year because of insufficient cash or cash flow problems. You can do a much better job of managing your business's finances if you have a handle on your cash inflows and outflows. Let's look at some of the basic concepts of financial accounting.

- **Assets** — Things of value held by the business. Examples include cash, accounts receivable, inventory, equipment and real estate.

- **Liabilities** — Amounts your business owes to creditors. Includes accounts payable, payroll taxes payable and loans payable.

- **Equity** — The net worth of your company. This is also called owner's equity or, in a corporate setting, paid-in capital. Equity results from investment in the business by its owner, plus accumulated net profits that haven't been paid out to the owner. In a sense, it is the amount owed by the business to the owner.

- **The accounting equation** — Assets = liabilities + owner's equity. The financial statement called the balance sheet is based on this equation.

- **Balance sheet** — Also called a statement of financial position, a balance sheet is a financial snapshot of the business at a given point in time. It lists your assets, your liabilities and the difference between the two, which is your equity or net worth.

- **Debits** — An increase in assets, or a decrease in liabilities or equity. In most American accounting systems, you will see debits entered into the left-hand side (the asset side of the accounting equation) of a two-column ledger or journal.

- **Credits** — An increase in liabilities or equity, or a decrease in assets. Generally, credits are entered into the right-hand side (the liability and equity side of the accounting equation) of a two-column ledger or journal.

- **Double-entry accounting** — In this type of accounting system, every transaction *always* has two journal entries: a debit and a credit. The debits and credits must always be equal, which prevents some common bookkeeping errors. It also makes it easier to find errors that do occur. We recommend new business owners adopt this system.

Example

John's painting business paints a new house on October 1, on credit, for one of the builders with whom he's established a relationship. His sales and cash receipts journal would contain a $3,000 debit entry, which would represent the account receivable (asset account) due from the builder. The journal would also contain a $3,000 credit entry to the painting revenue account (an income account). These two entries, taken together, show that accounts receivable has increased by $3,000, and that painting revenue has increased by the same amount.

When the builder receives the invoice and pays John the $3,000 on December 1, the following two entries would be made in the sales and cash receipts journal. First, the cash account (an asset account) would be debited, indicating a $3,000 increase in that account. Second, $3,000 would be credited to the accounts receivable account, indicating that the account has decreased by that amount.

Example of Double-Entry Accounting

Date	Entry	Debit	Credit
Oct. 1	Accounts Receivable (builder)	$3,000	
Oct. 1	Painting Revenue		$3,000
Dec. 1	Cash	$3,000	
Dec. 1	Accounts Receivable (builder)		$3,000

- **Single-entry accounting** — Rather than dealing with debits and credits, some very small businesses just record one side of the transaction. In the preceding example, a single entry of $3,000 in revenue would be made in the sales journal, and a single entry of $3,000 would be made in the accounts receivable ledger.

- **Cash method accounting** — The method of accounting used by most individuals to track their personal finances. If you use the cash method for your business, income is recorded only as it is received from customers, and expenses are recorded only when they are actually paid.

- **Accrual method accounting** — Using this method, income is recorded when a sale occurs, even if you don't get paid at that time. Similarly, expenses are recorded when you receive goods or services, even if you don't pay for them until later. Small businesses that maintain an inventory must use the accrual method, at least for sales and purchases of inventory for resale.

Understanding Accounting

Basically, accounting is the method by which financial information is gathered, processed and summarized into useful financial statements and reports. The process monitors how much money is being paid out and how much money is coming in. These records are vital to managing your cash flow. Here's how an accounting system works to provide you with current information about your business's financial health.

- **Transactions** — The process generally starts with an individual business transaction. For example, you may order statistical or demographic information regarding the geographic area in which you hope to locate your business. Each such transaction is generally represented by one or more documents (e.g., an order form, an invoice, a canceled check, etc.).

- **Journals** — A record of each transaction is kept in chronological order in what is commonly referred to as a journal. When you open your business, you'll probably be using three journals:

  — a sales and cash receipts journal, in which you'll record amounts coming into your business

  — a cash disbursements journal, in which you'll record the amounts you pay out

  — a general journal, used to account for special entries at the end of an accounting period

- **Ledger** — The transactions recorded in the journals are grouped according to type in a ledger. Every transaction is recorded in both a journal and a ledger. For example, the ledger would group all transactions affecting inventory in one place, all payroll expenses in another, etc. At the end of the month, the ledger can be compared to the amounts recorded in the journals. They should match. If they don't, you know something hasn't been reflected properly.

- **Trial balance** — This is prepared at the end of an accounting period by adding up all the individual account balances in the general ledger. If the sum of debit balances doesn't match the sum of credit balances, you'll have to track down the error.

- **Financial statements** — These are prepared from the information contained in the trial balance.

Because you're in the process of establishing a new business, some of these steps won't involve a lot of work on your part. For example, you probably won't have any sales or cash receipts to report in the early pre-opening days. But you will have plenty of use for the cash disbursements journal. Whether you're investigating a business opportunity, having business cards printed, or buying necessary equipment and supplies, you'll have plenty of transactions to record in the cash disbursements journal.

Working with Your Accountant

The preceding material demonstrates why we so strongly recommend bringing an accountant on board as early as possible. Not surprisingly, many people are put off or confused by the basic accounting concepts and methodologies. That's where your accountant and, probably, an accounting software package come into play.

Work Smart

 Today, many software companies make inexpensive accounting packages designed expressly for small business owners. Anyone who watches television has probably seen ads for several competing products. Some of these products allow a business owner to make a single entry for each transaction, which the program then records in a double-entry bookkeeping format. This affords the user the simplicity of entering items once with the accuracy and built-in checks and balances of double-entry accounting.

Along with the generic accounting packages, there are several industry-specific software packages set up with the accounts typically found within a given industry. These can reduce the time it takes you to set up an accounting system.

When you select an accountant, be sure to get a recommendation for a software package to use. In many cases, software packages organize information in such a way that your accountant can work directly from your electronic files, thus saving your accountant time and you money. It's a lot easier to hand over a diskette than to carry around copies of all your ledgers and journals.

Also, consider whether you want to have the accountant actually set up your accounting system for you. An accountant can show you how to keep the necessary records and set up an account structure appropriate to your type of business.

In the startup phase, remember, you'll be tracking mostly amounts you spend, since income won't start rolling in until you actually open up shop. This affords you an opportunity to shake down your bookkeeping system and get familiar with how entries are made. Don't hesitate to consult with your accountant if there's something you don't understand. While accountants are generally used to helping with less routine tasks like closing the books, preparing financial statements and completing tax returns, they also can be a resource when you have difficulty figuring out how to book a particular transaction.

If all this accounting talk seems a bit daunting, don't be too concerned. Accounting software has taken much of the hard part of accounting and relegated it to the background. If you've been able to take care of your personal finances without too much difficulty, business accounting shouldn't present much more of a challenge. For now, just remember that you need to keep an accurate record of the expenses you incur to investigate and start your new business.

CASH NEEDS WHEN OPENING FOR BUSINESS

If you've been following the steps we've outlined so far, you may be ready to pull together all that financial planning and daydreaming you've been doing. When at all possible, have a firm written estimate for every anticipated expense. If this is not possible, don't be too conservative in your estimate of cash needs. It's better to have money left over, than not enough.

Ideally, you will have planned for every contingency, especially those unique to your particular industry. But chances are that something you hadn't planned for will pop up. Cover yourself by expecting the unexpected.

Here are the most common kinds of startup expenses that many small businesses face:

Common Cash Requirements — Startup Phase

- ***Advertising and marketing promotion expenses*** — *You'll want to prime the pump by scheduling some advertising to appear before you officially open for business, and you may want to plan for a "grand opening" promotion as well.*

- ***Beginning inventory*** — *For retailers, this is the amount of inventory you will need to have in place on the first day you open the doors for business. This could be your most significant startup cost, so make sure you get an accurate estimate. Your suppliers, if you know who they will be, should be able to provide you with some help on required inventory levels for your type of business.*

- ***Cash*** — *Include the amount of money you'll need to run the cash register.*

- ***Decorating*** — *This will include cosmetic improvements to the new business facility. Usually, it is possible to get bids and ideas from interior decorators, who will give you a cost estimate even if you ultimately do the decorating yourself.*

- **Deposits** — *Include all amounts required by utilities and telephone companies. The utilities will be able to provide you with an estimate based on the business you operate.*

- **Fixtures and equipment** — *Include all fixtures and equipment needed for your new business. Finance this amount on a long-term basis if possible.*

- **Hiring employees** — *Although most employees won't start to work until you actually open, you may want to hire a key employee earlier to help with the initial tasks.*

- **Installing fixtures and equipment** — *This should be the amount necessary to make all the fixtures and equipment ready for use.*

- **Insurance payments** — *Ordinarily, the first premium is due when you purchase the policy. You will need liability and property insurance to protect yourself and any business assets. Depending on your business, you may also need some or all of the following: workers' compensation, health, life, disability, key person, business interruption, product liability and professional malpractice.*

- **Lease payments** — *Include amounts that must be paid for equipment and facility leases before opening. Expect to pay several months' worth of lease payments before you open the doors.*

- **Licenses and permits** — *This amount will include all fees charged by local, state and federal agencies. If your new business is in a highly regulated industry, expect these charges to be somewhat expensive. For example, an elder-care facility or a company handling toxic substances will have substantially higher fees than a clothing store.*

- **Professional fees** — *If you form a partnership, limited liability company or corporation, you'll probably need the assistance of an attorney in drawing up the proper documents and filing them with the state. You may also want to pay an accountant to set up your books.*

- **Remodeling** — *If your new business location will require any remodeling, include the cost here. Contractors will usually provide free bids after you have the plans drawn up. Don't forget to consider the cost of developing a design and creating the plans.*

- **Signs** — *Signage costs can be substantial. Obtain bids from sign companies. Finance this amount through long-term borrowing, if possible, or it will hurt your short-term cash flow.*

- **Supplies** — *Include all office, cleaning and employee supplies needed to stock the facility.*

- **Unanticipated expenses** — *A good rule of thumb is to compute the unanticipated expenses as 10 percent of the total cost of your money needed for startup.*

Startup Cash Needs Worksheet

On this page, we've provided a worksheet for itemizing all of these various startup expenses. Remember, be sure to carefully research each of the costs by getting estimates or talking with someone familiar with the matter. You don't want any surprises or shortfalls.

Worksheet 1: Initial Cash Requirements for a New Business
One-Time Startup Expenses

Startup Expenses	Amount	Description
Advertising	$	Promotion for opening business
Beginning inventory	$	Products or materials needed to open
Building construction	$	Amount per contractor bid
Cash	$	Requirements for the cash register
Decorating	$	Estimate based on bid
Deposits	$	Check with the utility companies
Fixtures and equipment	$	Amount per contractor bid
Install fixtures and equipment	$	Amount per contractor bid
Insurance	$	Amount per agent quote
Lease payment	$	Balance due before opening
Licenses and permits	$	Check with city or state offices
Professional fees	$	CPA, attorney, engineer, etc.
Remodeling	$	Amount per contractor bid
Rent	$	Balance due before opening
Services	$	Cleaning, maintenance, etc.
Signs	$	Amount per contractor bid
Supplies	$	For office, cleaning, etc.
Unanticipated expenses	$	Estimate for unexpected costs
Other	$	Costs unique to business
Other	$	Costs unique to business
Other	$	Costs unique to business
Other	$	Costs unique to business
Total Startup Dollars	$	

Work Smart

As you work through these expenses, don't forget that your accountant can be a great source of information regarding startup cost estimates. If the accountant has small business experience, he or she should be able to tell you whether your estimates are on target.

CASH NEEDS FOR THE FIRST 90 DAYS

Many new business owners plan only for their cash flow needs up to the day they open for business. But you also need to take a close look at the costs for the first 90 days of operation, since most businesses will take at least that long to build up a reliable stream of revenue.

The amount you need to keep the business running, called working capital, will vary by the type of business you own. If your business is a one-employee consulting firm, you will have a much smaller working capital requirement than a retail establishment with a large inventory.

Example

Assume your new business is a retail establishment selling furniture, and as a promotion, you plan to give buyers 90 days to pay. Your working capital needs could be enormous.

First, you have to buy your inventory; then, after it sells, you must pay for the replacement inventory. Your payment policy could mean you will not receive one dollar to pay bills for at least 90 days after you open the doors. If you do not plan for this working capital need in advance, you may not even stay in business for 90 days.

A good rule of thumb is to have access to enough working capital to pay all of your bills, except inventory purchases, for the first three months of operations. Inventory purchases will follow the special rules noted below.

Listed below are the most common cash requirements needed to keep a business open for the first 90 days.

Common Cash Requirements — The First 90 Days

- ***Advertising*** *— How much to spend on advertising depends on the type of business and the amount of competition. If you will be opening a retail establishment and plan to get your competitor's customers, your advertising budget will have to take that into account. You may be able to figure the approximate amount that should be spent on advertising from trade publications. Your advertising may be any combination of coupons, direct-mail, flyers, brochures, newspaper, radio or television.*

- **Bank service charges** — *These usually aren't a significant amount, but your bank should be able to give you an idea of how much to budget per month for these charges. Some banks will charge you for every check you deposit and every check you write on your business account.*

- **Credit card fees** — *These fees are usually based upon card usage. Normally, the costs are about 3 to 5 percent of the total charges. If you intend to allow your customers to buy your product or services by credit card, and you expect your business to have high credit card usage, allow for charges of 3 percent of sales in the price of your product or service. A chief benefit of credit card sales is the immediate business bank account deposit made electronically at the end of each day, making same-day payment a reality for any business doing credit card sales. This is especially advantageous if 30-day or longer payment terms can be arranged for inventory suppliers and other vendors.*

- **Delivery charges** — *These charges are for the cost of having inventory delivered to you. When you arrange for your inventory purchasing, ask about delivery charges.*

- **Dues and travel expenses** — *These expenses will vary by type of business. If you are in a regulated or professional industry, the expenses will be higher. For most retailers, trade association dues are nominal, but travel expenses may be substantial for the many regional and national trade shows.*

- **Interest** — *If you will be financing your new business with loans, compute the expected interest payments in your working capital needs.*

- **Inventory** — *When planning your working capital needs, include the additions to inventory for which you will not immediately receive cash. If inventory purchases are to replace inventories from cash sales, do not include them in your working capital budget.*

- **Lease payments** — *Include the amount that will be paid for equipment and facility leases in the first 90 days of your new business.*

- **Loan payments** — *This is the principal amount related to interest, above.*

- **Miscellaneous** — *Use this category as a catch-all for unanticipated costs and miscellaneous items you will incur during the first 90 days.*

- **Office expenses** — *These are various types of costs associated with running your business. They include paper, postage, photocopy expenses, etc.*

- **Payroll other than owner** — *If you'll have employees, compute the amount you will incur in the first 90 days of your business, by multiplying the number of employees that will be required for each hour, by the expected hourly rate, times the number of hours.*

- **Payroll taxes** — *These include Social Security and Medicare tax, and the federal and state unemployment tax. Generally, the total employer's share of Social Security and Medicare tax is 7.65 percent of payroll unless you will be paying people more than $68,400; at that point, a different set of rules will come into play. Unemployment rates vary on a state-by-state basis.*

- **Professional fees** — *In many cases, the largest professional fees will be incurred before you open the doors. In this category, include fees for accounting, consulting or payroll services you may need.*

- **Repairs and maintenance** — *In the first 90 days of your new business, this amount should be minimal, particularly if you are using new equipment.*

- **Salary of owner or manager** — *Remember to include 90 days' worth of your own salary, if you intend to draw a salary, as well as 90 days' worth of a manager's salary, if you intend to hire a manager.*

- **Sales tax** — *This varies on a state-by-state basis. The customer normally pays all sales taxes; however, you will have to pay sales tax on supplies, equipment and other items your business uses in its operations.*

- **Supplies** — *Include the amount you intend to spend on supplies in the first 90 days of your new business.*

- **Telephone charges** — *Check with your local phone company for the business rates. If your business will consist of high telephone usage, get bids from several different carriers.*

- **Utilities** — *Include all utilities your business will require, such as electricity, gas, water, sewer and refuse collection. These amounts can be estimated by the applicable carriers.*

First 90 Days Cash Needs Worksheet

On the next page, you'll find another worksheet that can help you to compute your initial cash requirements for the new business. This worksheet is a companion to the one for figuring startup costs, except it can help you estimate your on-going monthly expenses for the first 90 days of operation. Used in tandem, these worksheets can give you an accurate picture of your new business's financial situation.

Worksheet 2: Initial Cash Requirements for a New Business
Repeating Monthly Expenses for First 90 Days

Expenses	Amount	Description
Advertising	$	
Bank service charges	$	
Credit card fees	$	
Delivery charges	$	
Dues and subscriptions	$	
Health insurance	$	Exclude amount from Worksheet 1
Insurance	$	Exclude amount from Worksheet 1
Interest	$	
Inventory	$	See note 1, below
Lease payments	$	Exclude amount from Worksheet 1
Loan payments	$	Principal and interest payments
Miscellaneous	$	
Office expenses	$	
Payroll other than owner	$	
Payroll taxes	$	
Professional fees	$	
Rent	$	Exclude amount from Worksheet 1
Repairs and maintenance	$	
Salary of owner or manager	$	Only if applicable
Sales tax	$	
Supplies	$	
Telephone	$	
Utilities	$	
Other	$	
Total Repeating Expenses	$	
Total Startup Expenses (from Worksheet 1)	$	
Total Cash Needed	$	

[1] Include the amount needed for inventory expansion. If inventory is to be replaced from cash sales, do not include here. Assume that sales will generate sufficient cash for the replacements.

CASE STUDY OF SMALL BUSINESS COSTS

To further illustrate how cash is spent during startup and the first 90 days, we've taken the worksheets one step further and applied them to a fictitious new small business. Suppose you want to open a sub sandwich shop in Cedar Rapids, Iowa.

Here's a look at the startup dollars you'll need to get this business off the ground.

Case Study: Startup Dollars Needed

Item	Detailed Description	Amount
Beginning inventory	Includes food per bid from distributor	$1,500
Building construction	Leasing existing building	0
Cash	Only need cash for register	300
Decorating	Included in remodeling below	0
Deposits	$400 electric and $100 phone	500
Fixtures and equipment	Includes bids on all equipment	15,500
Franchise costs	Fees, training, signage, and supplies	4,000
Installing fixtures and equipment	All per bids	2,500
Insurance	Bids from the insurance carrier	3,000
License and permits	Includes sales and restaurant permits	750
Miscellaneous	Design fees on remodel	1,000
Professional fees	Cost for attorney to set up a corporation	1,000
Promotion:	Quarterly newspaper ads	1,500
	Monthly hotel room "town guide" listings	1,200
	Six flyer handouts	600
	Frequent diner program	500
	Electric exterior sign	2,500
Remodeling	Cost of leaseholder improvements per bid	8,000
Rent	Deposit of three months' lease payments	7,500
Services	Set up accounting system	500
Signs	Bids for inside and outside signs	1,000
Supplies	Cost of office and employee supplies	500
Unanticipated expenses	Computed 10 percent of the total cost	5,385
Total startup costs	**This is to get to day one of the business**	**$59,235**

Remember, this is only the dollars needed to get to day number one of opening this new business. Also, when using financing for the new business, you should match asset life with length of loans if possible. For example, on equipment with a five-year life, it would be preferable to obtain a five-year loan that matches the equipment life.

Now let's compute the continuing expenses of our fictitious sub shop for the first 90 days in business.

Case Study: Working Capital Needed for First 90 Days

Item	Detailed Description	Amount
Advertising	Budgeted newspaper and shopper at $200/month	$600
Bank service fees	Not a significant fee in this type of business	100
Credit card fees	Credit cards will not be accepted	0
Delivery charges	Amount included in inventory costs	0
Dues and subscription	Trade magazines for analyzing restaurant trends	50
Health insurance	Employ retirees and high school kids, no insurance	0
Insurance	All business insurance including worker's compensation	450
Interest	Loan for $60,000 at 10 percent, interest for 90 days	1,500
Inventory	This is an expansion of food inventory	1,000
Lease payments	Oven leased at $300 per month	900
Loan payments	Interest only due the first 90 days	0
Miscellaneous	Amount for contingencies	1,000
Office expense	Minimal office expense	100
Payroll-employees	Estimated	12,012
Payroll taxes	Is 10 percent of payroll	1,201
Professional fees	Consult with lawyer and accountant	600
Rent	Building at $1,000 per month per bid	3,000
Repairs and maintenance	Expect minimal based on new equipment and lease	200
Salary of owner	Owner has saved enough cash and wife works	0
Sales tax	Cash sales, sales tax is paid by customer	0
Supplies	Internet fees and various charges	100
Telephone	Business rate of $100 per month	300
Utilities	All utilities estimates for 90 days	1,200
Total	**Working capital needed for the first 90 days**	**$24,313**

The total amount needed to cover the continuing expenses of this sub shop for the first three months after opening its doors is $24,313. Added to the startup total of $59,235, the overall cost to open and operate this fictitious sub shop for three months is $83,548.

FORECASTING SALES

To get an accurate read on how much money you'll need to keep your business running in the first 90 days, you can't just look at the costs. You'll also need to figure out how much revenue your business will produce in those 90 days.

In an ideal world, your revenues would take care of all your expenses (and then some), and you wouldn't have to figure out how much more you'll have to pay out of your pocket to keep the business going. It might happen, but probably not within the first few months of operation.

Estimating your sales will be an inexact science. Don't count too heavily on your projections, and if you're going to err, do it on the conservative side in predicting how much business you'll do in your first 90 days.

If you have significant experience in the type of business and are familiar with the local economic conditions, your prior knowledge may give you the best estimate, but you still may want to back up your knowledge with outside verification from trade associations or financial information providers like Dun & Bradstreet.

MANAGING YOUR CASH FLOW

Inherent in the idea of figuring your costs is the need to understand the concept of cash flow. If you fail to satisfy a customer and lose that customer's business, you can always work harder to please the next one. But if you fail to have enough cash to pay your suppliers, creditors or your employees, *you're out of business!* No doubt about it, proper management of your cash flow is a very important step in making your business successful.

Simply stated, cash flow is the movement of money in and out of your business.

If you were able to do business in a perfect world, you'd probably like to have a cash inflow (product or service sold) occur every time you experience a cash outflow (expense paid). But business takes place in the real world, and things just don't happen like that.

Instead, cash outflows and inflows occur at different times. More often than not, inflows lag behind your outflows, leaving your business short of money. Think of this money shortage as your cash flow gap.

Profit vs. Cash Flow

If a retail business is able to buy a retail item for $1,000 and sell it for $2,000, then it has made a $1,000 profit. But what if the buyer is slow to pay his or her bill, and six months pass before the bill is paid? Using accrual accounting as we recommend, the retail business still shows a profit, but what about the bills it has to pay during those six months? It will not have the cash to pay them, despite the profit earned on the sale.

As you can see, profit and cash flow are two entirely different concepts. Profit is somewhat narrow, looking only at income and expenses at a certain point in time. Conversely, cash flow is more dynamic. It is concerned with the movement of money in and out of a business, and, more importantly, the time at which the movement takes place. You might even say the concept of cash flow is more in line with reality!

Cash Flow Variables

To properly manage your business's cash flow, you must first analyze the components that affect the timing of your cash inflows and outflows. A good analysis of these components will point out problem areas that lead to cash flow gaps for your business.

- **Accounts receivable** — Accounts receivable represent sales not yet collected as cash. In the worst case scenario, unpaid accounts receivable will leave your business without the necessary cash to pay its own bills. More commonly, late-paying or slow-paying customers will create chronic cash shortages. To offset this problem, consider reducing your average collection period, which will lower your investment in accounts payable and improve cash flow.

- **Trade discounts** — Some businesses allow customers to take a trade discount off the original sales price if the customer pays within a specified (shortened) period of time. The main advantage is it reduces the average collection period. The primary disadvantage is the cost to your bottom line profit associated with the lost revenues. The cost of trade discounts must be weighed against the improved cash flow expected.

- **Inventory** — This represents an investment of your business's cash that cannot be used for other purposes. Typically, a business purchases inventory and either pays for it at the time of the purchase or within 30 days. Depending on the nature of your business, it may be days or weeks before the inventory is resold, or used in the manufacturing of a final product and then sold. To offset this problem, consider reducing the average time you hold inventory by analyzing your turnover rates, which will lower your investment in inventory and improve cash flow.

- **Accounts payable** — These are amounts you owe to your suppliers sometime in the next 30 to 90 days, representing eventual outflows of cash. By delaying as long as possible and increasing your average payable period, you take full advantage of your trade credit and improve your own cash flow. But be careful not to ruin your credit or working relationship with suppliers. And by all means, pay your bills on time, but never before they are due.

Cash Flow Budgeting

A cash flow budget is a projection of your business's cash inflows and outflows on a month-to-month basis. Because of the uncertainty involved in the cash flow budget, trying to project too far into the future may prove to be less than worthwhile. A six-month budget minimizes the amount of uncertainty involved and also predicts future events early enough for you to take corrective action.

Preparing a cash flow budget involves four steps: preparing a sales forecast, generally based on last year's sales figures; projecting your anticipated cash inflows; projecting your anticipated cash outflows; and putting the projections together to come up with your cash flow bottom line.

> *Beginning Cash Balance*
> *+ Projected Cash Inflows*
> *− Projected Cash Outflows*
> ---
> *=* **Your Cash Flow Bottom Line (the ending cash balance)**

The ending cash balance for the first month becomes the second month's beginning cash balance. The second month's cash flow bottom line is determined by combining the beginning cash balance with the second month's anticipated cash inflows and cash outflows. The ending cash balance for the second month then becomes the third month's beginning cash balance. This process continues until the last month of the cash flow budget is completed.

Work Smart

The cash flow budget is an excellent tool to help you determine when you should or should not make major purchases. If your cash flow budget shows that additional funds may be available at a certain point, this should provide you with the opportunity to make advance purchase decisions. Planning ahead may allow you to take advantage of lower prices, discounts or better financing options. Likewise, if your cash flow budget shows your cash supply might be a little tight, it's probably not a good idea to make a major purchase or take on an additional monthly loan payment.

Any business, large or small, may experience a cash flow gap from time to time—it doesn't necessarily mean the business is in financial trouble. Cash flow gaps are often filled by external financing sources. Revolving lines of credit, bank loans and trade credit are just a few of the external financing options available for your business.

On the following pages, we've included a cash flow budget worksheet to be used for estimating the monthly inflows, outflows and bottom lines over a six-month period. Remember, when filling in the worksheet, the cash ending balance for one month becomes the cash beginning balance for the next month.

Cash Flow Budget Worksheet			
	Month 1	*Month 2*	*Month 3*
Cash beginning balance	$	$	$
Income:			
Accounts receivable collections	$	$	$
Loan proceeds	$	$	$
Sales & receipts	$	$	$
Other:	$	$	$
+ Total cash inflows	$	$	$
Expenses:			
Advertising	$	$	$
Bank service charges	$	$	$
Credit card fees	$	$	$
Delivery	$	$	$
Health insurance	$	$	$
Insurance	$	$	$
Interest	$	$	$
Inventory purchases	$	$	$
Miscellaneous	$	$	$
Office	$	$	$
Payroll	$	$	$
Payroll taxes	$	$	$
Professional fees	$	$	$
Rent or lease	$	$	$
Subscriptions & dues	$	$	$
Supplies	$	$	$
Taxes & licenses	$	$	$
Utilities & telephone	$	$	$
Other:	$	$	$
Subtotal expenses:	$	$	$
Capital purchases	$	$	$
Loan principal	$	$	$
Owner's draw	$	$	$
Other:	$	$	$
Subtotal other outflows	$	$	$
– Total cash outflows	$	$	$
Cash ending balance (short)	$	$	$

Cash Flow Budget Worksheet

Month 4	Month 5	Month 6	Total
$	$	$	$
$	$	$	$
$	$	$	$
$	$	$	$
$	$	$	$
$	$	$	$
$	$	$	$
$	$	$	$
$	$	$	$
$	$	$	$
$	$	$	$
$	$	$	$
$	$	$	$
$	$	$	$
$	$	$	$
$	$	$	$
$	$	$	$
$	$	$	$
$	$	$	$
$	$	$	$
$	$	$	$
$	$	$	$
$	$	$	$
$	$	$	$
$	$	$	$
$	$	$	$
$	$	$	$
$	$	$	$
$	$	$	$
$	$	$	$
$	$	$	$

Some Final Words

If, at times, the tone of this book sounds a little discouraging, do not be put off by our words. That is not our intent. In fact, our hope is that we have pointed out all of the various concerns that must be considered when launching your first small business. We want to make sure you have every opportunity to succeed.

Yes, it is a challenging and sometimes difficult process. Owning a small business takes a lot of money, time and effort. But it's far from impossible to undertake. Just look around. Successful small businesses are everywhere.

And these businesses provide more than just personal wealth and satisfaction for their owners (although, if that's all they provided, that wouldn't be too bad). According to recent government statistics, small businesses are the lifeblood of this country's economy, employing the majority of the private work force and producing nearly two-thirds of the new jobs created in the last year.

Moreover, entrepreneurship is the source of most innovation. New ideas, different ideas, great ideas—all of these ideas generally start small, and then rise, evolve or fall on their own merits. And small businesses serve as the incubators for these ideas. After all, Microsoft's Bill Gates started out by writing computer programs for his local school district when he was a teenager. A few years later he developed and sold a yet unknown operating system called DOS to the technological giant IBM. The rest is, well . . . you know the rest.

The point is that you can succeed in small business. You just have to be willing to do your homework. And that's where we come in. We hope we've pointed you in the right direction. And as you run and grow your new operation, feel free to call on us for additional information.

In fact, the goal of this book is to get you thinking about what it takes and if you are the right type of person to become a first-time business owner. If you believe that you're ready to make it happen, we highly suggest that your research should continue with our other, more in-depth offerings on small business subjects.

The *CCH Business Owner's Toolkit* on the Internet (www.toolkit.cch.com) is a complete information database available free of charge to small business owners or would-be entrepreneurs. Business tips, interactive advice, worksheets, tools and news items are all there at your disposal, 24 hours a day.

And be sure to check out our library of book titles available online or at a bookstore near you. They also offer guidance on many of the primary subjects of interest affecting business owners. Some of the titles include:

- ***Start Run and Grow a Successful Small Business***—our all-in-one, soup-to-nuts reference guide on entrepreneurship

- ***Business Plans That Work for Your Small Business***—detailed coverage of business planning, complete with five real-life sample plans

- ***Small Business Financing: How and Where To Get It***—the ins and outs of handling business finances and raising capital

- ***Safe Harbors: An Asset Protection Guide for Small Business Owners***—a higher-level resource for structuring, funding and operating a business with minimal risk to personal and business assets

- ***Find and Keep Customers for Your Small Business***—a marketing primer that improves sales through better customer outreach

- ***Win Government Contracts for Your Small Business***—make the government your best customer

- ***CCH Business Owner's Toolkit Tax Guide***—our annual publication that ensures business owners get every break or advantage coming to them, lowering their tax bills

So while the majority of the burden for success falls on you, just remember that you're not alone. We're here to help.

Good luck!

Index

. . . *Formulating and Writing an Effective Business Plan?*

Business Plans That Work for Your Small Business now in its second edition-clearly translates complicated marketing and financial concepts into down-to-earth practical advice, explains all the essential elements and formulas, and offers concrete examples throughout. Five newly developed sample plans from real small businesses provide readers with the blueprints for their own plans, as well as a wealth of detailed information about how a successful small business should operate.

This book will appeal not only to budding entrepreneurs who are planning a new venture on paper to see whether it will fly, but also to new or existing business owners who need a business plan document as part of a business loan application, and to established owners who want to create a plan for internal use.

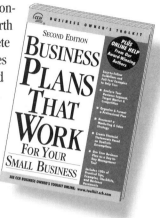

304 pages / Book No. 0-5246-200 **$19.**⁹⁵*

. . . *Making the Government Your Best Customer?*

All government contracts under $100,000 are targeted to small businesses. ***Win Government Contracts for Your Small Business***—now fully updated in its second edition—will show you how to get in on the action in just 10 easy-to-understand steps. By following our practical advice, you'll be accurately listed in the federal procurement system, allowing you to start receiving bids right away.

In this book you'll learn the simple most important step to take before you start bidding, where to find government buyers, the best source of bid leads for you and your company, how to write a winning proposal, listings of essential web sites, and how to use the Internet to your advantage. All together, this is the only book that covers, step-by-step and in detail, how to successfully compete for government contracts—and make more money for your small business.

$19.⁹⁵* *506 pages / Book No. 0-5352-300*

. . . *Securing the Necessary Financing for Your Business?*

Small Business Financing: How and Where To Get It, now in its newly revised second edition, thoroughly but simply discusses each source of debt and equity capital, whether public or private—from bookstrapping and IPOs to commercial loans and SBA-guaranteed programs, and everything in between. This book covers methods for determining the amount of capital needed, choosing an appropriate source and type of financing, selecting a business form, and planning successful applications or presentations.

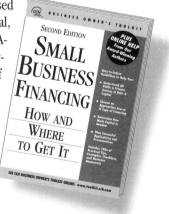

Sample forms are integrated into the text to facilitate learning the details and the data-gathering skills needed for the financing process. A handy glossary is included to take the mystery out of dealing with bankers and other financial professionals.

224 pages / Book No. 0-5142-200 **$17.**⁹⁵*